NATURE IN A NUTSHELL FOR KIDS

Over 100 Activities You Can Do in Ten Minutes or Less

Jean Potter

JOHN WILEY & SONS, INC.

New York • Chichester • Brisbane • Toronto • Singapore

Copyright © 1995 by Jean Potter
Published by John Wiley & Sons, Inc.

Library of Congress Cataloging-in-Publication Data

Potter, Jean.
    Nature in a nutshell for kids : over 100 activities you can do in
ten minutes or less / Jean Potter.
        p.   cm.
    Includes bibliographical references and index.
    ISBN 0-471-04444-X (paper)
    1. Nature study—Activity programs—Juvenile literature.
[1. Nature study.]   I. Title.
QH54.5.P67   1995
508'.078—dc20   94-28953

Printed in the United States of America

10   9   8   7   6   5

This book is dedicated to
Karen W. and Fred L. Haddad,
our dear friends.

Special thanks to:

Thomas, my husband, for his undivided love and support.
Archie, our Welsh Corgi, for patiently waiting outside every day.
Shadow, our cat, for staying by my side each day.
Mary, for her constant guidance, love, and support.
Kate Bradford, my editor, for her excellent comments and friendship.
Mom, Dad, Kathy, and Emmett for their unconditional love.

Contents

Spring

Summer

Autumn

Winter

Introduction

Nature in a Nutshell for Kids contains 112 quick and easy activities that will help you discover the beauty and wonder of the natural world, from trees and plants to insects and spiders. Each activity takes only ten minutes or less to complete. Soon you will be able to plan your own adventures as you solve many of the mysteries of nature and learn about how the natural world works.

HOW THIS BOOK IS ORGANIZED

Each season brings new opportunities to know nature, so this book is divided into sections that can be identified by a graphic symbol:

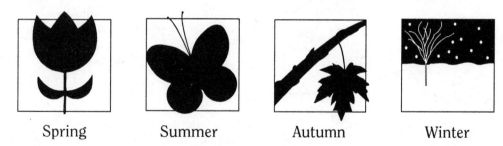

| Spring | Summer | Autumn | Winter |

Also, if you are looking for a particular topic, such as insects, plants, or weather, you can find it in the Activity Index at the back of the book.

Each activity answers a particular question about nature and includes a list of the materials you need, easy-to-follow steps, and an explanation of what the activity demonstrates. There is no need to buy special materials, but you may want to visit the library for additional information on the topic.

TIPS FOR COMPLETING THE ACTIVITIES

Try to be very careful as you complete your observations and explorations. These tips will help:

Be prepared. Read through any activity before you begin to do it. Collect all the materials required before you start, and place them in the order in which you will use them.

Be accurate. When conducting your activities, follow directions closely, and write down all results.

Be creative. After completing an activity according to the directions, try to think of ways that you can change the activity. Look for the results from your change to the activity. But before you make the change, ask an adult if your substitution is all right. This will help ensure safety and also avoid wasting materials.

Be careful. Ask for adult assistance and supervision when using sharp instruments. Materials should be used for the purpose for which they were intended. Work cautiously.

Be neat. Keep your work and your work area as neat as you can. Use clean instruments, and wash them after every use. Always put your materials away clean.

KEEPING A NATURE NOTEBOOK

Learning about nature is a lifelong adventure, so it is a good idea to keep notes of your nature studies. Your nature notebook does not need to be elaborate. It can be a notebook or a file on your computer. You simply want a place to record your observations and findings.

For each investigation, you will want to include several categories in your nature notebook:

Date. The date will not only tell you when the nature study was conducted, but it can provide you with valuable information about your findings during a particular time of the year. This information will be helpful when you want to study the same topic at a later date or on the same date the following year.

Time. The time of day or night you study nature can be significant. Many things in nature change quite a bit depending on whether they are observed in the daytime or at night.

Weather. Your activities may be affected by the weather. Record the temperature; cloud formations; rain, snow, and wind conditions; and other weather information. By maintaining good records, you may be able to predict how nature is affected by the weather.

Location. The location of your nature study is important. It is usually not enough to just record, "my backyard." Try to be more specific about the location: "on the right side of the front porch next to the knothole." Then if you need to find the location again, you will be able to go directly to it. Keep in mind that the outdoor environment is constantly changing. Record the location from different directions, and use lots of landmarks in your description.

Description of procedure. The description of your study should be detailed. It is always better to have more information than not enough. Do not rely just on your memory to fill in the missing information. You would be surprised at how much you can forget in several months.

Illustrations. Drawings are an important part of recording information. You do not need to be a great artist to draw maps, plants, or animals. You just need to be able to interpret what you have written and drawn.

TIPS FOR STUDYING NATURE

Getting close to nature also means helping to care for and maintain it. If you do, nature will continue to be as beautiful as it is for a long time.

Observe natural beauty. Each season offers a new and different look at the world. Stop to enjoy the beauty of every season.

Be curious. Studying nature requires a keen awareness of your surroundings. Keep your eyes open, and watch for unusual occurrences and changes. Ask yourself and others questions about things you do not know. Record any questions that remain unanswered in your nature notebook.

Always ask permission to study nature. Regardless of where you are studying nature, be sure to obtain permission before taking any natural materials. Consult your parents or another adult before cutting branches or picking flowers, and ask others for permission to study and take materials from their property.

Never damage any plant unnecessarily. When you walk through natural areas, be careful not to break branches or step on wildflowers.

Take only what you need. If an activity requires you to take something from nature, collect only enough to complete the project. When you observe insects and other animals, do not harm them, and return them to the place where you found them.

Leave natural things the way you found them. When you turn over a rock to inspect the underside, put the rock back the way you found it.

Clean up litter. When you are finished in an outdoor study area, leave it cleaner than you found it, if possible. Take any litter you find to a trash can or recycle it.

SPRING

 With the arrival of spring, the days grow warmer and longer. Clouds travel through the skies, sometimes picking up water droplets. When enough water droplets gather, it rains. The raindrops find their way through the small openings in the soil, nourishing roots and seeds. Well-rested trees begin to grow, and their buds begin to burst forth.

Sunshine warms the soil as seeds begin to grow. Gardeners tend their vegetables and flowers. Soon new green sprouts peek out of the earth looking for the sun's energy to help them grow into mature plants. Crocuses are some of the first flowers to bloom and are followed by petals on the daffodil the color of sunshine.

Baby animals are born in the spring. They have plenty of food to eat to help them grow. Baby birds soon leave their nests looking for worms to eat. Tiny tadpoles emerge from frog eggs in warm and shallow ponds.

Squirrels and chipmunks explore their environment looking for food. Rabbits begin to scurry about looking for the gardener's plantings. Earthworms begin to poke their heads out of the darkness of the earth. Flocks of ducks and birds fly north where they will find food. Bees buzz, birds chirp, hummingbirds flutter about, and lawn mowers roar. The joys of experiencing spring fever make everyone's spirits rise.

ACID RAIN

What Are the Effects of Acid Rain?

MATERIALS

white chalk
plastic cup
1 teaspoon (5 ml) white vinegar

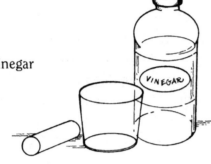

PROCEDURE

1. Place the white chalk in the plastic cup.
2. Pour the vinegar on the chalk. What happens to the chalk?

EXPLANATION

Chalk is made of **limestone.** Limestone is a rock that reacts to the acid in vinegar. When you poured the vinegar on the chalk, the chalk gave off a gas, which you saw as lots of bubbles. **Acid rain** contains a very weak acid that it collects from polluted air. When acid rain falls on limestone, some of the rock is eaten away. Acid rain can also poison our lakes, rivers, and streams.

CLOSED CONES

How Do Pinecones React to Wet Weather?

MATERIALS

two pinecones from a white pine or hemlock pine
bowl of tap water
timer

PROCEDURE

1. Place one pinecone in the tap water for 10 minutes.
2. Keep one pinecone dry. What happens to the wet pinecone in comparison to the dry one?
3. Let the pinecone dry out and inspect it again.

EXPLANATION

After a few minutes, the wet pinecone's scales started to close. Pinecones rely on the force of the wind to blow their seeds to a spot where they can grow. Therefore, the seeds must be light and as dry as possible. During rainstorms, the pinecones act as little umbrellas to keep the seeds dry. When the pinecone dries, it opens again.

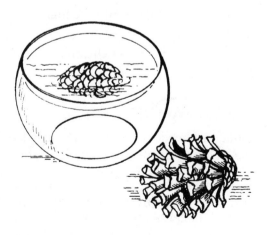

CLOUD CREATION

How Are Clouds Formed?

MATERIALS

rubber stopper that fits the jug
nail
hammer
gallon (3.8 liter) jug
warm tap water
adult helper

PROCEDURE

1. Have an adult helper make a hole in the stopper using the nail and the hammer.
2. Rinse the jug with warm tap water.
3. Insert the stopper into the jug.
4. Blow as much air as you can through the stopper hole.
5. Put your finger over the hole immediately, and do not let any air escape.
6. Pull the stopper out quickly. What do you see?

EXPLANATION

Clouds are made up of tiny water droplets floating in the air. Clouds form when warm, moist air meets cooler air. In the cooler air, the water vapor **condenses,** or becomes a liquid. When you blew into the bottle, you filled it with warm, wet air from your lungs. This air was at a higher temperature and **pressure** (the amount of force pressing on an area) than the surrounding air. When you opened the bottle, the cooler, low-pressure air rushed in, and some of the water vapor turned back into liquid water, forming a cloud.

8

CLOUD PREDICTIONS

What Do Different Types of Clouds Mean?

MATERIALS

clouds

PROCEDURE

1. Lie on your back and observe the clouds.
2. Read the descriptions below and determine what types of clouds are in the sky.
3. Study the clouds and determine what is going on in the atmosphere.

EXPLANATION

Clouds are large clusters of tiny water droplets in the air. Clouds will look different depending on conditions in the atmosphere. When you watch the clouds build and move along, you might be able to predict the type of weather that is coming. **Cirrus clouds** are the highest clouds. They are made entirely of ice crystals, so that sometimes you can see the stars shining through them. They usually indicate snow or rain. **Stratus clouds** are low hanging. They are so spread out that they often resemble fog. They stretch across the sky in long, horizontal layers and develop when cold air cuts under warm, moist-filled air. They often produce long, steady rains or snow. **Cumulus clouds** are fluffy, cauliflower-shaped clouds with flat, broad bases. Usually they form on top of rapidly rising currents of warm air. These clouds form on clear days.

STRATUS CLOUDS

CIRRUS CLOUDS

CUMULUS CLOUDS

CROCUS LIGHT

How Does a Crocus Flower React to the Lack of Light?

MATERIALS

blooming crocus
shoe box
timer

PROCEDURE

1. On a sunny day, find a blooming crocus and look at the petals carefully.
2. Cover the flower with the shoe box for 5 minutes.
3. Remove the box and look at the petals. What happened to them?

EXPLANATION

All plants and flowers react to sunlight, but with some the reaction is more obvious. A sunflower always faces the sun and moves very slowly, following the sun. Crocus flowers are also very sensitive to light. When you covered them with the box and shut out the light, the crocus closed its petals. When you removed the box only a few minutes later, the petals slowly opened. You can also see the crocus close its petals later in the day when the sun goes down.

DUCK FEATHERS

How Do a Duck's Feathers React to Rain?

MATERIALS

eyedropper
tap water
goose or duck feather (from
    a pillow or collected from
    the ground near a pond)
magnifying lens

PROCEDURE

1. Fill the eyedropper with tap water.
2. Place a few drops of water on the feather.
3. Use the magnifying lens to observe the feather. What happens to the water drops?

EXPLANATION

Feathers serve two main purposes. They keep birds warm, and they enable them to fly. Each feather has tiny hairlike sections called **barbs.** Each barb has many tiny hooked **barbules,** or hairlike branches, that connect to other barbules on either side like the teeth of a zipper.

The barbs are covered with an oily substance, made in the duck's skin, that keeps water away from the duck. When you put the water from the eyedropper on the feather, the water just rolled off.

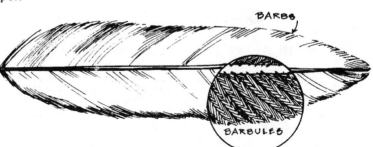

BARBS

BARBULES

11

EARTHWORM OBSERVATIONS

How Do Earthworms Behave?

MATERIALS

2 earthworms
paper towels
magnifying lens
ice cube
soil

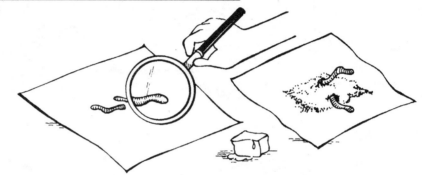

PROCEDURE

1. Find the earthworms at night or after a rainfall because that is when they come out of the ground.
2. Lay the earthworms on a moistened paper towel.
3. Using the magnifying lens, watch the worms move around.
4. Touch one worm with the ice cube and watch how it reacts.
5. Cover the worms with a paper towel for a few minutes to block out the light.
6. Lift the paper towel to expose the worms to the bright light and watch how they react.
7. Put a mound of soil on a paper towel and place the worms on it. Watch them again. When you have finished the activity, return the worms to the place where you found them.

EXPLANATION

Earthworms live underground where it is dark and damp. They tunnel their way through the earth and generally come out at night. They avoid direct sunlight, but have no eyes. Instead, they have a pair of spots that are sensitive to light. When you covered the worms with a paper towel, they probably did not move until you removed the towel. When you touched the worm with an ice cube, its whole body reacted. This is because each **segment** (section) of an earthworm's body has at least one pair of nerve endings that are very sensitive to cold.

EASY ECOSYSTEM

How Can You Make an Ecosystem?

MATERIALS

soil
aquarium
sand
rocks
green plants
twigs and sticks
crawling insects (ants, beetles, caterpillars)
earthworms
screen
masking tape

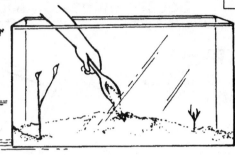

PROCEDURE

1. Place the soil in the bottom of the aquarium.
2. Add the sand and rocks.
3. Position the green plants so they will be easy for the insects to climb on and under.
4. Add an arrangement of the twigs and sticks.
5. Add the crawling insects and earthworms one at a time.
6. Place the screen on top of the aquarium.
7. Tape around the screen so it stays in place. Watch the insects and plants adapt to the environment. What happens in the ecosystem you created?
8. When you have finished observing the ecosystem, release the insects in the places where you found them.

EXPLANATION

The earth is an **ecosystem,** an environment of plants and animals living together. In any ecosystem, the balance of living things is important. Plants must provide food and oxygen for the animals, and the animals must provide **carbon dioxide,** a colorless gas, and nutrients for the plants. This process of **recycling,** or reusing, is constant in an ecosystem.

ECOLOGY INCH

What Can You See in a Few Square Inches of Your Environment?

MATERIALS

empty picture frame
magnifying lens

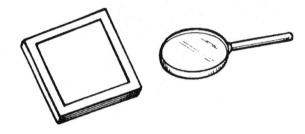

PROCEDURE

1. Pick an interesting outdoor area, such as a patch of grass or weeds.
2. Lay the picture frame on the ground to frame the area you have chosen.
3. Use the magnifying lens to examine the mini-environment.
4. Watch for interesting insects, plant life, and soil features. How do the insects interact with one another? With plants? With soil?

EXPLANATION

Ecology is the study of how people and animals interact with their environment. Understanding an area's ecology gives you an appreciation of why we need to conserve wildlife and care for the environment. As you studied the few square inches of the environment you chose, you learned more about plants and animals and how they behave.

EROSION SLANT

How Does the Slant of the Land Affect Erosion?

MATERIALS

masking tape
2 milk cartons
scissors
soil

4 wooden blocks
2 baking pans
small sprinkling can
tap water

PROCEDURE

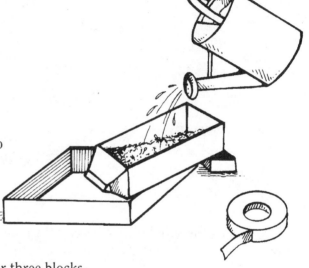

1. Tape the opening of each milk carton closed.
2. Cut away the entire front panel of each carton to form a large opening.
3. Lay the cartons down with the open sides facing up. Put enough soil in the cartons so they are almost full.
4. Prop the top end of one carton on one of the wooden blocks.
5. Prop the top end of the other carton on the other three blocks.
6. Lay the bottom ends of the cartons in separate baking pans.
7. Using the sprinkling can, water the soil in the carton that is propped up on one block. Observe the water.
8. Refill the can and sprinkle the water on the soil in the carton propped up on three blocks. Observe the water. How did the water trails compare, and which baking pan collected more run-off soil?

EXPLANATION

Rain sometimes carries soil from one place to another. The wearing away of rock and soil is called **erosion.** Faster-moving water carries more soil. So during a hard rain, more soil is washed away. The water moved faster through the milk carton propped on the three blocks, and more soil ran off into the baking pan.

EROSION STOPPER

How Can Erosion Be Prevented?

MATERIALS

sand
soil
aquarium
twigs
small sprinkling can
tap water

PROCEDURE

1. Mix the sand and soil together in the aquarium.
2. Form the soil into a mound.
3. Stick the twigs into the soil on one side of the mound to represent trees and plants.
4. Using the sprinkling can, water the mound as if it were raining fairly hard on both sides of the mound at the same time. What happens to each side of the mound?

EXPLANATION

Erosion is the process of wearing away rock or soil. Plants anchor their roots in the earth, which helps prevent the soil from washing away. The twigs represented plants anchored in soil. More soil was left on the side with the twigs when you watered the mound. Most of the soil on the side without the twigs washed away. Trees and other plant life prevent soil from washing away when it rains.

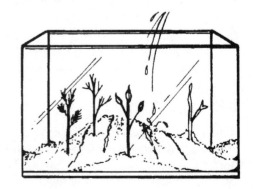

FLIGHT PATTERN

What Are the Different Flight Patterns of Birds?

MATERIALS

binoculars
pencil
sheet of notebook paper
field guide to birds

PROCEDURE

1. Observe the flight patterns of different birds through the binoculars.
2. Record the type of bird and its flight pattern.
3. In the field guide, read about the flight patterns of the birds you observed.

EXPLANATION

Birds have different ways of flying depending on the shape of their wings. Broad wings give a bird a good lift for slow flight or for rapid takeoff. Tails enable birds to maneuver around. Some birds, like eagles, have wide-spread feathers and long wings, which help them glide and soar in the air for hours. Pheasants have short, broad wings, enabling them to make quick takeoffs and steep climbs.

HARD WATER

How Does Water Affect the Ability of Soap to Clean?

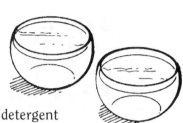

MATERIALS

2 clear plastic bowls
rain water
tap water
2 teaspoons (10 ml) Epsom salts
4 tablespoons (60 ml) powdered laundry detergent

PROCEDURE

1. Collect rain water in one of the plastic bowls.
2. Put tap water in the second bowl.
3. Mix the Epsom salts into the tap water.
4. Add the laundry detergent to each bowl of water and mix. In which bowl does the detergent dissolve better?

EXPLANATION

By adding the Epsom salts to the tap water, you caused the water to become hard water. **Hard water** contains lots of **minerals,** or compounds that make up rocks. Rain that has just fallen is considered soft water because it has not collected minerals from the earth. It is easier for suds to form in soft water because soft water does not contain minerals. In hard water, the chemicals in the soap combine with the minerals in the water to form soap scum. This soap scum sticks to the side of the tub or to your hair.

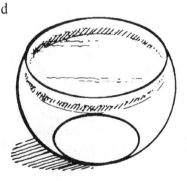

INVESTIGATING EGGS

What Is Inside an Egg?

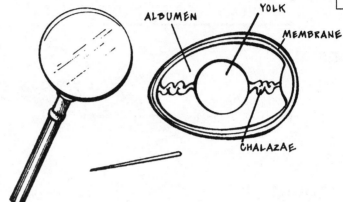

MATERIALS

chicken egg
magnifying lens
bowl
toothpick

PROCEDURE

1. If the egg was in the refrigerator, let it sit out for a while to warm.
2. Examine the outside of the egg under the magnifying lens.
3. Slowly crack the egg open over a bowl and examine the inside of the shell under the magnifying lens.
4. Study the inside of the egg. Notice the membrane inside the shell.
5. Examine the other parts of the membrane. Feel the white jelly material.
6. Examine the yolk. What is the thin membrane around the yolk holding it in a round shape?

EXPLANATION

A chicken egg is a single cell that contains its own food. The white or brown hard surface, the shell, is part of the protective **membrane** that surrounds the inside of the egg. When you cracked the egg open, you saw the membrane clinging to the inside of the shell. The membrane acts as a layer of insulation between the shell and the inside of the egg. The yellow center of the egg is the yolk, which is the food source for the developing chick. The yolk is held in place by two spiral bands of protein. These bands, called **chalazae,** hold the yolk in place on top of the growing chick. The white part of the egg is called the **albumen.** The albumen contains water reserved for the chick and holds the yolk.

NEST BUILDING

What Materials Do Birds Use to Build Nests?

MATERIALS

wire clothes hanger
mesh potato (or onion) bag
scrap materials (strips of fabric,
    yarn, string)

PROCEDURE

1. Bend the wire into a diamond shape.
2. Slide the mesh bag onto the hanger and tie the bag at the top.
3. Weave short pieces of fabric, yarn, and string through the mesh.
4. Suspend the wire hanger from a tree and watch what happens.

EXPLANATION

In the spring, birds look for materials with which to build nests. Birds build their nests from the materials they find in nature, such as twigs and grasses. But they also use manufactured items, like fabric, yarn, and string, if they find them. Later, you can try to find the nest made from your scrap materials.

POND INSPECTION

What Kinds of Living Things Can Be Found in Pond Water?

MATERIALS

pond water
plastic pail
clear plastic bowl
magnifying lens
adult helper
You must have access to a pond.

PROCEDURE

1. With your adult helper, carefully scoop up some pond water with the plastic pail.
2. Pour the water into the plastic bowl.
3. Use the magnifying lens to inspect the materials in the bowl. What do you see?

EXPLANATION

After a few moments, the heavier materials fell to the bottom of the bowl, and you were able to see some of the things that live in the water. Weeds, insects, and other tiny water creatures, such as **hydras,** are generally found in pond water. You may even have scooped up a tadpole or a small fish. Some of the living things may be too small to see even with a magnifying lens. If you have a microscope, try putting some of the pond water on a slide to see if you can spot any more creatures moving around. When you are finished with your inspection, return your water creatures and the remaining water to the pond.

21

RAINDROP PRESERVATION

How Can You Save a Raindrop?

MATERIALS

flour
pan
rain water
slotted spoon
baking pan
adult helper
You must have access to an oven.

PROCEDURE

1. Spread the flour in the pan so it is about 1 inch (2.5 cm) thick.
2. Take the pan outside and hold it in the rain.
3. After several raindrops fall onto the flour, bring the pan inside.
4. Sift out the floured raindrops with the slotted spoon.
5. Place the small wet flour pieces in the baking pan.
6. Ask your adult helper to bake the raindrops at 350 degrees until they are hard.

EXPLANATION

When you held the flour in the rain, you captured the raindrops falling through the air. The drops of water soaked into the flour to form hard pellets. After baking, the flour hardened and created a raindrop model.

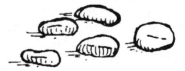

SEED EMBRYO

What Are the Parts of a Seed?

MATERIALS

lima bean	knife
plastic cup	magnifying lens
tap water	adult helper

PROCEDURE

1. Place the lima bean in the plastic cup.
2. Add enough tap water to cover the bean.
3. Let the bean soak for about 5 minutes.
4. Have your adult helper cut the bean open lengthwise. Examine the inside with the magnifying lens. What do you see?

EXPLANATION

Inside every seed is a miniature plant, or **embryo.** Seeds contain enough food for the embryo to grow until it can make its own food. Seeds have three important parts. The outer skin that protects the seed is called the **seed coat.** The food supply inside the seed is called the **endosperm.** The **cotyledons** are the first leaves the plant produces.

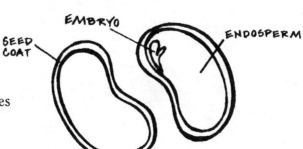

SOIL CREATION

How Is Soil Created?

MATERIALS

sheet of white paper
two rocks
magnifying lens

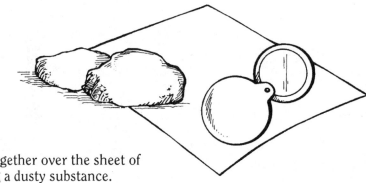

PROCEDURE

1. Rub the two rocks together over the sheet of white paper, creating a dusty substance.
2. Examine the dust under the magnifying lens.

EXPLANATION

Soil is made up of plant and animal debris and of tiny pieces of rock. Sometimes rocks are broken by ocean waves or by river and creek water washing over them. Sometimes the wind blows across rocks, loosening the top layers. Sun and rain slowly cause rocks to crumble. The dust you made by rubbing the two rocks together could be one component of soil.

SOIL MOISTURE

How Much Water Can Soil Hold?

MATERIALS

can opener	potting soil
2 soup cans	4 cups (1,000 ml)
2 washcloths	tap water
2 rubber bands	pail
2 pie plates	ruler
spoon	adult helper
sand	

PROCEDURE

1. Have your adult helper cut off both ends of each soup can.
2. Wrap a washcloth around the bottom of each can and secure it to the can with a rubber band. Be sure the rubber band holds it tightly in place.
3. Place each can on a pie plate with the washcloth end down.
4. Spoon the sand into one of the cans three-quarters of the way up.
5. Spoon the potting soil in the second can three-quarters of the way up.
6. Gently shake each can so the sand and soil settle, and there are no air holes.
7. Slowly pour 2 cups (500 ml) of the tap water on top of the sand.
8. Slowly pour 2 cups (500 ml) of the tap water on top of the soil.
9. After 5 minutes, carefully remove the cans and set them in the pail.
10. Measure and record the amount of water that passed through the sand and potting soil into the pie plates. Which material allowed more water to pass through it?

EXPLANATION

Water moves through different kinds of soils at different speeds. The larger the soil particles, the faster the water passes through. Sand particles are uneven and do not fit together, so there are many air holes between them. There is less space between the soil particles, so the water does not pass as rapidly through the soil as it does through the sand.

25

SOIL SAMPLE

What Is in Soil?

MATERIALS

fresh soil
2 sheets of white paper
desk lamp
tweezers
magnifying lens

PROCEDURE

1. Lay the soil on one of the sheets of white paper under the desk lamp.
2. With the tweezers, filter through the soil to find tiny pieces of rock, animal, and plant debris.
3. Inspect the particles under the magnifying lens and try to determine what they are.
4. On the second sheet of paper, sort the findings according to what you think they are.

EXPLANATION

Fresh soil contains many different particles. These particles include tiny pieces of rocks, animals, and **humus,** which is organic matter made of dead plants and animals. All of these have broken down into very small pieces but may not be completely **decomposed,** so you can see what some of the particles once were. The **organic matter** (from a living thing) in soil provides plants with nutrients.

SPINNING SPIDER

What Types of Webs Do Spiders Weave?

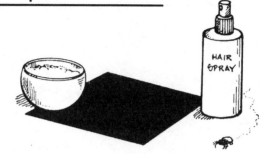

MATERIALS

spider web
flour
sheet of black construction paper
hair spray

PROCEDURE

1. Find a spider web early in the morning. Be sure the spider is not on the web.
2. Lightly shake a small amount of flour on the web.
3. Hold the sheet of construction paper behind the web.
4. Press the paper carefully against the web so as not to break the web.
5. Lift the paper away and find an impression of the web.
6. Spray the impression with hair spray to protect it. Look carefully at the design the spider wove. What type of design did it imprint?

EXPLANATION

Spiders spin elaborately patterned webs. They secrete a liquid from the back of their bodies that turns into a solid thread when it hits the air. When a spider begins weaving, it begins at the center, then builds spokes that point out from the center in all directions. Finally, the spider spins the strands around the spokes to form the web. The strands contain a sticky substance that holds any insect which comes into contact with the web. The spider feels the insect trapped in its web by the vibrations the insect's movements send along the strands of the web.

There are three main types of webs. The garden spider builds an **orb web,** which has spoke formations, as in a bicycle wheel. These webs are generally found outside. The **sheet web** is flat and is generally built indoors by house spiders. Sheet webs are usually found in corners. The **funnel web** looks like a circle of wires wrapped around one another. Funnel webs are found among dead leaves on the ground.

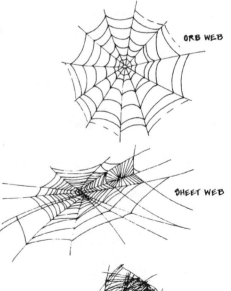

ORB WEB

SHEET WEB

FUNNEL WEB

27

SPRING HUNT

What Are Some of the Signs of Spring?

MATERIALS

pencil
sheet of notebook paper
magnifying lens
binoculars

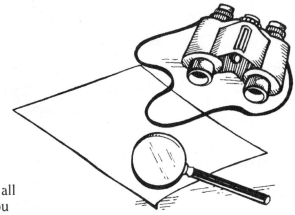

PROCEDURE

1. On the sheet of paper, list all the signs of spring that you can think of.

2. Take your list, the magnifying lens, and the binoculars outdoors and check off the signs of spring that you find.

EXPLANATION

Spring brings new awakening and excitement to the environment. Some signs of spring are birds looking for food and building nests; buds appearing on plants; seedlings beginning to grow; crocuses and daffodils blooming; earthworms surfacing after a rain; and insects crawling, flying, and buzzing everywhere.

TORNADO MIX

How Does a Tornado Spin?

MATERIALS

jar with a screw-on lid
tap water
3 drops blue food coloring
1 teaspoon (5 ml) dishwashing liquid

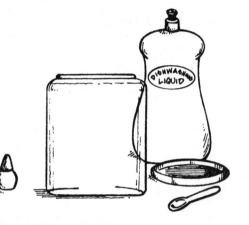

PROCEDURE

1. Fill the jar with tap water, leaving only about 1 inch (2.5 cm) of space at the top.
2. Add the blue food coloring.
3. Add the dishwashing liquid.
4. Screw the lid on very tight.
5. To make the tornado, hold the jar horizontally in front of you with both hands.
6. Swirl the jar straight in front of you in a smooth, fast, and circular motion about 12 to 15 times.
7. Immediately turn the jar up the right way. What happens when you turn the jar right-side up?

EXPLANATION

Tornadoes are high-speed winds that violently spin in a funnel shape. They travel across the surface of land, causing tremendous destruction. The water in the jar demonstrated the motion of the wind in a tornado. The circular energy in the water pulled the water to the outside, while the less dense air took up the space the water occupied.

WATER CYCLE

How Does the Water Cycle Work?

MATERIALS

soil
plastic zip bag
tap water
masking tape

PROCEDURE

1. Place the soil in the bottom of the plastic bag.
2. Sprinkle just enough tap water on the soil to dampen it.
3. Close the bag so it is tight and tape it to a sunny window.
4. Observe the bag for the next few minutes. What happens in the bag?

EXPLANATION

The water in our environment moves in a cycle. When it rains, water falls and soaks into the earth or runs into waterways. When water on the earth is heated, it turns into water vapor and is carried around in the air. The water partially evaporates. This vapor condenses in the atmosphere and forms clouds, which produce rain. As the sun warmed the soil in the bag, you saw water droplets form at the top of the bag. When enough water collected at the top, it became heavy and fell back to the soil like rain.

30

WATER QUALITY

Is Rain Water Pure Water?

MATERIALS

coffee filter
plastic cup
rubber band
rain water

PROCEDURE

1. Place the coffee filter over the mouth of the plastic cup.
2. Put the rubber band around the filter to keep the filter in place.
3. Press a small dent in the middle of the filter so the water will drain well.
4. Place the cup in the rain to collect rain water.
5. After the rain, remove and examine the filter. What do you see?

EXPLANATION

When you inspected the filter, you saw some dark specks and perhaps some smudges on it. The water passed through the filter, but other particles did not. Water in the air picks up dirt and dust particles. When the water falls back to earth, it takes these particles with it. Sometimes the particles are harmful, as in the case of acid rain. Acid rain is caused by the release of gases and other matter into the atmosphere from factories and engines and from natural occurrences like volcanoes and other sources. The chemicals in these materials mix with rain water and change its make-up.

WET SOIL

Why Is the Best Garden Soil a Mixture of Elements?

MATERIALS

sand
clay soil
peat
4 large plastic bowls
sprinkling can
tap water

PROCEDURE

1. Take equal amounts of sandy soil, clay soil, and peat. Place each material in a separate bowl.
2. In the fourth bowl, mix together the same amounts of the sandy soil, clay soil, and peat.
3. Sprinkle tap water slowly into each of the bowls. What happens to the water in each of the materials?

EXPLANATION

Sand is composed of small particles that do not fit tightly together. The spaces between the bits of sand allow the water to pass through quickly. Plants in sandy soil do not get much water. In clay

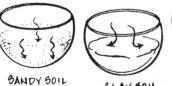

SANDY SOIL   CLAY SOIL

PEAT

SAND, CLAY, and PEAT

soil, particles cling together closely. The water cannot get through, so it collects on top. The roots of plants in clay soil do not get much water. Peat absorbs and holds some water, letting the rest pass through. Plants in just peat do not get enough water. In the mixture in the fourth bowl, the sand and peat help loosen the clay and provide a way of maintaining water.

WINDY WEATHERING

How Does Wind Affect Soil?

MATERIALS

1 cup (250 ml) potting soil
1 cup (250 ml) fine gravel
1 cup (250 ml) sand
large balloon
ruler

PROCEDURE

1. Mix together the potting soil, gravel, and sand.
2. Pile the mixture on a flat surface such as a paved driveway.
3. Inflate the balloon and hold the neck so the air does not escape.
4. Hold the neck of the balloon about 6 inches (15 cm) from the soil mixture.
5. Let the air out of the balloon. What happens to the soil mixture?

EXPLANATION

The air from the balloon acted as a strong gust of wind. Winds are able to move large quantities of soil from one place to another. When you let the air from the balloon hit the soil, the smaller and lighter-weight soil particles blew away. The gravel did not move as much, if it moved at all. This is an example of **weathering,** or the wearing away of the earth by weather conditions like wind. One good place to see weathering on stone is in an old cemetery. Walk through a cemetery and pay close attention to the headstones and their dates.

These headstones are probably made of a hard stone like marble or granite. Notice that the older headstones have weathered a great deal more than the newer ones.

SMALL GRAVEL

SAND AND POTTING SOIL

SUMMER

 Summer is a time of growth. Young animals are hungry, and there is plenty of food for them to eat. Deer enjoy fresh green grass, and ducks find weeds, small seeds, and insects in the waters of lakes and ponds. Frogs stick their tongues out to catch and eat insects, worms, and snails.

Hummingbirds, butterflies, and bees sip nectar. Pollen is collected and passed from flower to flower in preparation for seed production. The wind blows ever so slightly to help in the pollination process.

Trees enjoy the abundance of light and grow rapidly. Their branches grow longer, and their leaves mature. Under the earth, roots are reaching out through the soil to collect the nutrients and water they need.

Gardens are lush and produce nutritious vegetables. Flowers are in full, beautiful bloom. And everyone enjoys the wonderful summer weather.

CHLOROPHYLL TEST

Why Is Grass Green?

MATERIALS

sheet of white construction paper
grass

PROCEDURE

1. Place the sheet of construction paper on the grass.
2. Step on the paper and twist your foot into the grass.
3. Lift the paper and examine it. What do you see on the paper?

EXPLANATION

You saw green smudges on the paper where the grass rubbed on the paper. Grass and other plants are green because they contain a pigment called **chlorophyll.** Chlorophyll is vital to plants. Plants cannot move around to get food, so they must make it themselves. Plants make food from carbon dioxide (found in the air), water, and sunlight through the process of **photosynthesis.** Without chlorophyll, this process could not take place.

DENSE DIP

Why Is It Easier to Float in the Ocean Than in a Swimming Pool?

MATERIALS

2 clear plastic bowls
tap water
food coloring
10 tablespoons (50 ml) salt
spoon
2 eggs

PROCEDURE

1. Half fill both plastic bowls with tap water.
2. Add a few drops of food coloring to the water in one bowl.
3. Mix the salt into the colored water.
4. Stir until the salt is all or mostly dissolved.
5. Place an egg in each bowl of water. What happens to the eggs?

EXPLANATION

The egg in the salt water floated, but the egg in the fresh water sank to the bottom. If the egg in the salt water did not float, keep adding salt to the water until it does. Salt water is **denser** (the particles in it are closer together) than fresh water. The egg floated because the density of the egg was less than the density of the salt water. It is easier for you to float in the ocean than in fresh water for the same reason. The ocean is full of salt, so it is denser than fresh water.

FIREFLY EXAM

What Are Fireflies?

MATERIALS

jar with air holes in lid
fireflies
magnifying lens

PROCEDURE

1. Choose a night when fireflies
   are out. Capture some fireflies in the jar. Look for variations of color, rang-
   ing from yellows to greens.
2. Observe the fireflies under the magnifying
   lens for a few minutes to see if you can
   follow their blinking patterns.

EXPLANATION

A firefly, also called a lightning bug, is
really a type of beetle that uses light to
attract its mate. Fireflies have a special
organ under the body that causes the
light to turn on and off. When they
light, they give a signal to
their mates. Fireflies start
signaling at dusk and continue until late in the
evening. They can be seen
from midsummer to early autumn.

FISH AGE

How Can You Determine the Age of a Fish?

MATERIALS

dead fish, from a fresh fish market
magnifying lens

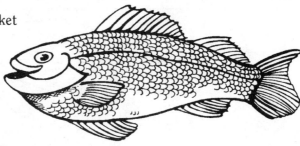

PROCEDURE

1. Lay the fish flat on a table.
2. Look at its scales under the magnifying lens.
3. Find the parts of the scales that resemble clusters and count them.

EXPLANATION

The scales on a fish form within weeks after hatching. They are protection for the fish, but you can use these scales as a way of telling the age of the fish. The scales have round, bony ridges, called **circuli,** which show the growth pattern of the fish. This part of the scale is embedded in the skin and has clusters of ridges around it. Each cluster represents one year of growth. To determine the age of the fish, just count the clusters around each scale.

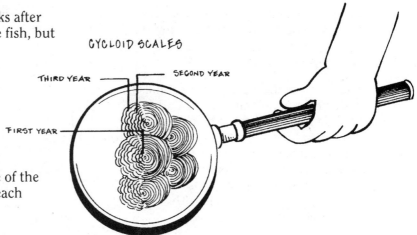

CYCLOID SCALES

THIRD YEAR

SECOND YEAR

FIRST YEAR

FLOWER EXAMINATION

What Are the Parts of a Flower?

MATERIALS

flower in bud
magnifying lens
flower in bloom

PROCEDURE

1. Examine the flower bud under the magnifying lens.
2. Notice the small green parts that hold the bud on the stem.
3. Look carefully at the flower in bloom. The most obvious and colorful parts are the petals.
4. Examine the inside of the petals and find any number of stamens.
5. Look in the center of the flower to find one or more sepals.
6. Finally, examine where the flower is attached to the stem. This part is known as the flower stalk. How do all of these parts work together?

EXPLANATION

The flower **stalk** is the part that holds the flower on the plant. The small green parts of the plant between the bud and the stalk are called **sepals.** They protect the bud until it opens to bloom, then they fall off.

When you looked inside the flower, you could see the parts that make the plant reproduce. The **stamens** are long tubes with knobs on the ends. The stamens produce pollen. The **pistil** makes the flower's seeds.

GREENHOUSE HEAT

How Do the Sun's Rays Warm a Greenhouse?

MATERIALS

masking tape
2 thermometers
2 pieces of cardboard slightly larger than
   the thermometers
jar with lid

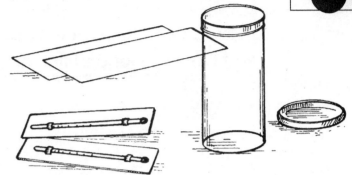

PROCEDURE

1. Tape each of the thermometers to a separate piece of cardboard.
2. Place one thermometer with the cardboard attached in a jar and put the lid on.
3. Place the jar on a windowsill.
4. Lay the second thermometer with the cardboard attached against the window facing the room. Be sure the sun does not shine directly on the faces of the thermometers.
5. Let the thermometers stand for several minutes. Then read the temperature on each thermometer. What are the differences in the temperature of the thermometers?

EXPLANATION

The temperature reading on the thermometer inside the jar was higher than the reading on the thermometer outside the jar. Light from the sun travels through the air in waves. Short **infrared rays,** or heat rays, from the sun pass through glass and warm objects. The warmed objects then give off rays of a longer wavelength. The shorter waves travel through the glass jar, but the longer waves do not. So the heat is trapped in the jar. This is how the sun warms a greenhouse.

41

GROUND TEMPERATURE

How Does the Temperature Above Ground and Underground Differ on a Hot Day?

MATERIALS

trowel
2 thermometers
piece of cardboard the size of one thermometer

PROCEDURE

1. Dig a hole in the ground.
2. Place one of the thermometers in the hole and cover it with the piece of cardboard.
3. Place the second thermometer on top of the ground in the sun.
4. Wait about 5 minutes and read each thermometer. What is the difference between the thermometer readings?

EXPLANATION

The temperature on the thermometer underground was lower than that on the thermometer above ground. On a hot day, the sun's rays warm objects above ground, but do not reach below ground. If you were to try this experiment on a cold day, the thermometer underground would probably be warmer than that above ground because it would be insulated by the soil from the cold air.

INSIDE SHELLS

What Does the Inside of a Shell Look Like?

MATERIALS

empty spiral shell
coarse sandpaper

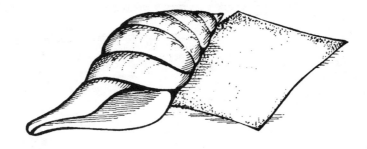

PROCEDURE

1. Examine the outside of the shell and observe the spirals.
2. Grip the shell tightly and rub it very hard against the sandpaper.
3. Continue to rub the shell to wear away one side. What do you see when you rub away most of the shell?

EXPLANATION

Some animals live inside shells that protect their soft bodies. The shells are usually hard and can be found in all sizes and colors. Shells found near the sea are generally made of a mineral called **calcium.** They no longer have an animal inside. When you wore away the side of the shell with the sandpaper, you revealed the inside of the shell. It has a spiral shape. As the organism grew, it added layers to the shell, which appear as rings on the outside of the shell.

LOW HUMIDITY

Why Do You Feel Cooler When the Humidity Is Low?

MATERIALS

plastic bowl of tap water
cloth
2 thermometers

PROCEDURE

1. Choose a sunny day with low humidity and take the materials outdoors.
2. Wet the cloth and wrap one end of it around the bulb end of one of the thermometers.
3. Place the other end of the cloth in the bowl of tap water so the thermometer hangs out of the bowl.
4. Place the second thermometer on the ground next to the bowl. Make sure both thermometers are in the sun. After a few minutes, read the thermometers. What are the readings?

EXPLANATION

The air always contains water, even though the water cannot be seen. **Humidity** is the measurement of the weight of water in a specific volume of air. If the air contains only a small amount of water, we say the humidity is low. When the humidity is low, water evaporates more easily because there is room in the air to absorb the water. As water evaporates, it takes heat from the object it comes into contact with. In your experiment, the water from the cloth evaporated and cooled the thermometer. This is why the temperature on the thermometer wrapped in the wet cloth was lower than that on the other thermometer.

MALE MOTHS

How Can Male Moths Be Attracted?

MATERIALS

2 teaspoons (5 ml) sugar
2 tablespoons (30 ml) tap water
small, shallow plate
shoe box
outdoor light
screen

PROCEDURE

1. After dark, mix the sugar with the tap water on the plate.
2. Put the plate inside the shoe box.
3. Place the box under the outdoor light.
4. Watch for moths to land in the box.
5. Close the moths in by placing the screen over the top of the box.
6. Without letting the moths out, remove the plate of sugared water.
7. Watch to see whether more moths come and land on the screen. What attracted these moths?
8. After you have completed the activity, remove the screen and let the moths fly away.

EXPLANATION

Moths usually fly in the evening or at night. They are attracted to light and to sweet things. They first fly to the light, then stay for the sugar water. Female moths give off a substance known as **pheromones** to attract mates. Male moths can smell the substance from as far as several miles away and will come to the source. This is why the box of moths attracted more moths, even without the sugar water.

MOON BRIGHT

How Does the Moon Shine?

MATERIALS

a friend
eyeglasses

PROCEDURE

1. On a sunny day, ask your friend to put on the eyeglasses.
2. Ask your friend to walk backward slowly while facing you until the eyeglasses reflect the sun. Your friend should look at you, *not* look directly at the sun. What happens when the sun reflects on the glasses?

EXPLANATION

Your friend's eyeglasses became very bright when the sun's light reflected directly off them. The moon also reflects the sun's light; it does not create its own light. The rocks on the surface of the moon are made of materials that reflect the light of the sun back to you on the earth. The portion of the moon that you see each night depends on the location of the sun in relation to the moon.

MOVING CURRENTS

What Causes Ocean Currents?

MATERIALS

clear plastic bowl
tap water
baby powder

PROCEDURE

1. Fill the plastic bowl with the tap water.
2. Sprinkle a tiny amount of the baby powder on the water.
3. Gently blow across the surface of the water and baby powder. What happens?

EXPLANATION

Sea water is constantly circulating in orderly patterns called **currents.** Continuous winds are the main force that keeps currents moving. Blowing on the surface of the water caused the water to start moving in circles. The baby powder made it easier for you to see the movement of the water. The water in the center of the bowl made ripples as it moved from the center outward. One circular movement went in a clockwise direction while the other went counterclockwise.

NIGHT SOUNDS

What Animals Make Sounds at Night?

MATERIALS

tape recorder
blank tape
timer

PROCEDURE

1. Find a rural or suburban area where you can be absolutely quiet and press "record" on your tape recorder.
2. As you record, listen to the sounds of nature and try to identify them.
3. Turn off the tape recorder after 5 minutes.
4. Bring your tape recorder inside and play the sounds.

EXPLANATION

Nocturnal animals are those that are mostly active at night. Raccoons, cats, mice, deer, and owls are some common nocturnal animals. If you listen carefully, you might hear an owl's hoot, a cat's meow, or the noise of a raccoon raiding a garbage can. Nocturnal animals are hidden by the darkness so they can better avoid predators or sneak up on prey. Most of these animals have very large eyes, so they can see in little or no light, and many have especially good hearing and sense of smell.

OCEAN FOAM

What Causes Ocean Foam?

MATERIALS

egg
cold metal bowl
kitchen whisk

PROCEDURE

1. Crack the egg open and separate the white from the yolk. The easy way to do this is by holding the half shells over the metal bowl and shifting the yolk back and forth between the shells, letting the white fall into the bowl.
2. With the whisk, beat the egg white until it turns to foam and stands in stiff peaks. What do the stiff peaks resemble?

EXPLANATION

The most common cause of surface waves on the ocean is the wind. The size of the waves depends on the wind speed, wind duration, and distance of water over which the wind blows. As the waves crash on the shore, millions of tiny bubbles form because lots of air mixes with the water. When you studied the foam of the egg white, you saw stiff peaks. These peaks form because you beat thousands of tiny air bubbles into the egg white, much as the wind beats air into ocean water.

SAND COLORS

What Color Is Sand?

MATERIALS

handful of sand
sheet of dark paper
magnifying lens

PROCEDURE

1. Place the sand on the sheet of paper.
2. Scatter the sand with your hand and look at the grains under the magnifying lens. What colors and variations of colors do you see?

EXPLANATION

When you looked closely at the grains of sand, you noticed that they were not all the same color. The color of each grain depends upon the materials form which the sand came. Quartz is **translucent** (light shines through it) white, tan, or yellow. Feldspar is gray or pink. Fragments of seashells are usually white and **opaque** (light does not shine through them). Some beaches even have black sand, which comes from volcanic ash.

SAND IMPRESSIONS

How Are Fossil Impressions Formed?

MATERIALS

sand
cake pan
tap water
seashells
package of plaster of paris
plastic bowl
plastic spoon

PROCEDURE

1. Pour the sand into the cake pan.
2. Moisten the sand with tap water until it is wet enough to hold an impression.
3. Make several impressions in the sand with the seashells.
4. Mix the plaster of paris in the plastic bowl according to the directions on the package.
5. Quickly pour the plaster into the sand impressions you have made. (*Note:* Throw the remaining plaster in the trash. Do not throw it in the sink because it will clog the drain.)
6. Let the plaster dry for a few minutes.
7. Remove the shells from the plaster. What do you see?

EXPLANATION

Fossils are the preserved forms or parts of plants and animals that lived many millions of years ago. **Impressions** are the shape of shells, bones, leaves, and other objects that were pressed into sand or mud. Most fossils and fossil impressions have been found near the sea. The plant or animal sank to the bottom of the sea bed and the soft parts rotted away. But the mud surrounding it as well as the hard shells and bones turned to rock.

SAND SECRETS

What Is Sand?

MATERIALS

dry beach sand
screen strainer
plate
magnifying lens

PROCEDURE

1. Place the beach sand in the strainer and shake most of the sand through.
2. Place the materials that did not shake through the sand on the plate and examine them under the magnifying lens. What do you see?

EXPLANATION

You were probably able to see small shells, pebbles, fish teeth, and bones that once belonged to animals that lived in the sea. These materials were broken into tiny pieces by the action of the ocean waves against the shore. As the waves receded because of the tide, these pieces were left on the shore.

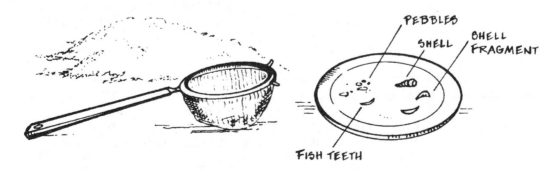

PEBBLES

SHELL

SHELL FRAGMENT

FISH TEETH

SECRET PLACE

What Can You Find Living Under a Rock?

MATERIALS

rock
magnifying lens
field guide to insects

PROCEDURE

1. Carefully turn over a rock that has been undisturbed for a while.
2. Look under the rock. Notice any insects that immediately rushed away when you turned the rock over.
3. Watch the animals to see where they are going and what they are doing.
4. Examine the soil beneath the rock with the magnifying lens. What do you find?
5. Use the field guide to determine which insects you found.
6. Put the rock back exactly as you found it.

EXPLANATION

Many insects live in dark, moist places. The soil just under rocks provides the perfect environment for these insects. The living things that you found under your rock were different depending upon the location of the rock and the time of year. Small insects seen under rocks might be ants, millipedes, centipedes, slugs, caterpillars, spiders, beetles, and sow bugs. When you turned the rock over, the insects and worms probably moved very quickly to escape the light. The pill bugs may have curled up as a defense mechanism. You may also have found some white insect eggs.

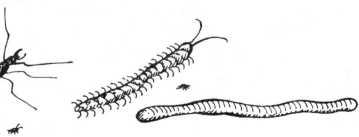

SEEKING LIGHT

Why Don't Leaves Grow on the Lower Parts of Trees in the Forest?

MATERIALS

forest area

PROCEDURE

Go for a walk in a forest area and look up at the tops of the trees. What do you notice about the leaves?

EXPLANATION

Most leaves on trees in the forest grow at the top. Trees must have light in order to produce food. In the forest, where many trees block out much of the light, each tree must struggle to find light. So you will see trees bending toward light and many leaves at the tops of the trees.

SHADOW WATCH

What Happens to Shadows After a Few Minutes?

MATERIALS

object
sheet of paper
red marking pen
blue marking pen

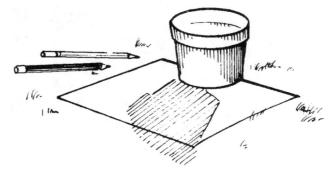

PROCEDURE

1. Put the object on the sheet of paper in the sun.
2. Draw an outline around the object's shadow with the red marking pen.
3. Leave the shadow for a few minutes.
4. Return to the shadow and draw an outline again with the blue marking pen. What do you notice?

EXPLANATION

A shadow is made when an object blocks the light rays falling on it. The shadow is approximately the shape of the solid object that blocks out the light, but the shadow will be longer or shorter depending on the angle of the light hitting the object. As the earth moves, the angle of the sun's light on the object changes, causing the shape of the shadow to change. When you left the shadow for a few minutes and then returned, you saw a difference in the shape of the shadow. This difference is an indication of how much the earth moved since you drew the shadow.

SINGING BIRDS

How Do Bird Songs Differ?

MATERIALS

pencil
sheet of notebook paper
field guide to birds

PROCEDURE

1. Find a quiet place in an area where birds can be found.
2. Sit for several minutes and listen to the songs of the birds. Can you distinguish one bird from another? Write down the bird calls you hear.
3. In your field guide, find a description of the sound each bird makes. Can you match these descriptions to your notes?

EXPLANATION

Birds have many distinguishing characteristics, including their calls. The American kestrel emits a shrill *klee-klee-klee.* The killdeer seems to say *killdee, kildee.* The mourning dove gives a soft *ooh-ah-woo-woo-woo,* and the great horned owl calls with a *whoo! whoo-whoo-whoo! whoo! whoo!* The American crow repeats a loud *caw-caw-caw.* The American robin sings a cheerful *cheerily-cheerily.* The American sparrow sings a *teedle eet, teedle eet,* while the chipping sparrow simply gives a *chip* call. You'll find many more bird songs described in your field guide and as you listen to birds in nature.

SNAIL STUDY

How Does a Snail Move Around?

MATERIALS

snail
clear plastic cup

PROCEDURE

1. Look for a snail in a moist outdoor area or at an aquarium store.
2. Gently pick up the snail and put it in the plastic cup.
3. Hold the cup in different ways so you can examine how the snail moves about.
4. Release the snail in the same location as you found it. What do you notice about the way the snail travels?

EXPLANATION

Snails are small **mollusks.** They have soft, segmented bodies with no bones, and they need to be moist to stay alive. Snails do not have legs, but move by gliding slowly on a layer of slime that oozes from their bodies. This substance leaves a trail on the plastic cup that you can easily see. If their environment becomes dry, snails secrete another fluid that closes them inside their shells until the environment is wet again.

57

SOIL LAYERS

What Are the Different Layers of Soil?

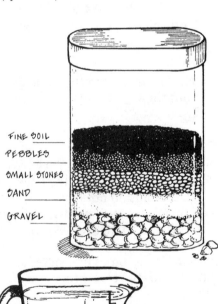

MATERIALS

sand
fine soil
fine gravel
pebbles

small stones
tall plastic jar with
   lid
tap water

PROCEDURE

1. Place small, equals amounts of the sand, fine soil, gravel, pebbles, and small stones in the plastic jar so the jar is half full.
2. Add tap water so the jar is three-quarters full.
3. Put the lid on so it is tight.
4. Shake the jar vigorously.
5. Let the jar stand and watch the materials settle. What happens after a few minutes?

EXPLANATION

Soil is a layer of small fragments of rocks, minerals, and plant and animal debris. It covers the earth and forms layers. The uppermost layer of soil is called **topsoil.** Topsoil is rich in nutrients because it contains the most organic matter. The layer of soil under the topsoil is called **subsoil.** It is lighter in color than topsoil and contains little organic matter. Water drains through the subsoil so that it does not stay in the topsoil and rot the plants. Beneath the subsoil is a layer of broken rock. The elements in your jar settled according to the weight of the materials, with the heaviest settling on the bottom. This is how the earth's soil settles into layers.

FINE SOIL
PEBBLES
SMALL STONES
SAND
GRAVEL

SPIDER LEGS

How Does a Spider Walk with All Those Legs?

MATERIALS

spider
magnifying lens

PROCEDURE

1. Locate a spider.
2. Hold the magnifying lens over the spider to watch the spider walk. What do you notice about its ability to coordinate all of its legs?

EXPLANATION

Spiders have eight legs. The four pairs of legs have to be slightly different lengths so they do not bump into one another as they sweep back and forth. The movements of each leg are coordinated with those of every other leg in a weaving sequence.

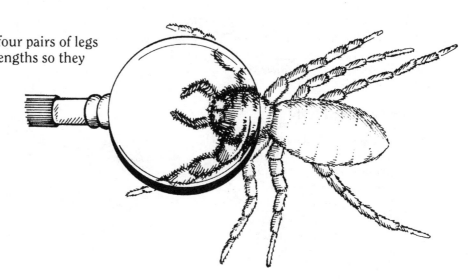

SUMMER EATING

What Types of Plants Do Insects Eat?

MATERIALS

field guide to insects
outdoor plants
magnifying lens

PROCEDURE

1. Use the field guide to identify the insects
   on the outdoor plants.
2. Inspect the plants under the magnifying lens to find insects or
   signs of insects (such as holes in the leaves). What
   insects did you find, or what signs of insect
   infestation did you see?

EXPLANATION

Plants are great places for insects
because they provide both food
and shelter. Each type of insect
prefers a different type of plant.
Leaf hoppers enjoy the sap
violets offer. Bumble bees can
be seen hovering around red
clover. Japanese beetles eat the
leaves of roses.

SWIM BLADDER

How Does a Fish Float?

MATERIALS

plastic tub (if you do not have access to a sink)
tap water
small plastic soda bottle with cap

PROCEDURE

1. Fill the sink with tap water.
2. Half fill the soda bottle with water and put the cap on.
3. Place the bottle in the sink. Notice that it floats.
4. Remove the bottle from the sink and uncap it.
5. Add water so the bottle is three-quarters full and replace the cap.
6. Place the bottle in the sink again. What happens to the bottle this time?

EXPLANATION

Buoyancy is the tendency of something to float. Some fish have an organ called a **swim bladder,** which is a long sac filled with air that lies just above the digestive system. The fish controls its buoyancy by varying the amount and pressure of the air in its swim bladder. You reduced the amount and pressure of the air when you added water to the bottle. The bottle that contained more air floated higher in the water.

WATER LAYERS

How Can One Kind of Water Float on Another?

MATERIALS

plastic tub
cold tap water
2 balloons of the same size and shape
hot top water

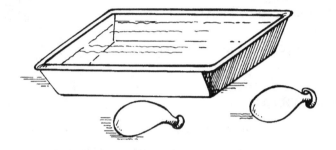

PROCEDURE

1. Fill the tub with cold tap water.
2. Almost fill one of the balloons with hot tap water.
3. Almost fill the second balloon with cold tap water.
4. Tie the balloons and place them in the tub. What happens to each balloon?

EXPLANATION

The balloon filled with hot water floated, but the balloon filled with cold water sank. Cold water is heavier than warm water because it is denser (the molecules are closer together). This is why sometimes when you are in the ocean, you can feel that the water around your chest is warm, but the water at your feet is cold.

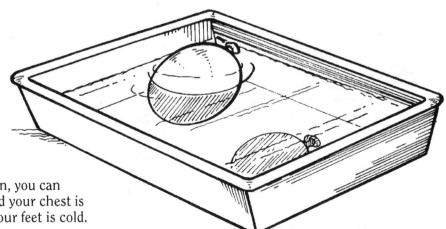

WIND WAVES

How Are Waves Made?

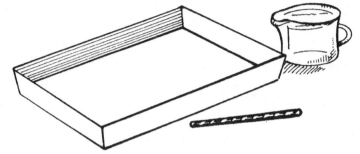

MATERIALS

large, shallow cake pan
tap water
drinking straw

PROCEDURE

1. Fill the cake pan with tap water.
2. Hold one end of the drinking straw close to the water.
3. Blow air through the straw on the water's surface, sometimes blowing hard and sometimes softly. What happens as you blow on the water?

EXPLANATION

By blowing on the water, you produced waves on the top of the water. The energy of the air pushes the water, creating waves. This energy increases as the speed of the air increases. The height of the waves changes according to the amount of air blowing on the surface. As the energy passes through the water, ripples of waves move through the water.

AUTUMN

 Autumn is marked by cooler weather and shorter days. Everyone and everything prepare for the cold weather ahead.

Chipmunks fill their cheeks with nuts as they store food for the winter. Squirrels scamper about searching for their winter stock. Woodchucks fill their bellies with grass and leaves, gaining fat so their bodies will be warm enough to sleep all winter. Animals begin growing thick winter coats. Many kinds of birds prepare for a long migration south.

Insects lay eggs for spring hatching. Ants tunnel through the darkness of the earth, where they have already collected and hidden food. Bees that have gathered nectar during the summer now hide in hollow trees, making honey for winter nourishment.

Trees stop growing as the light diminishes. Their leaves begin to turn brilliant red, yellow, and orange and will soon turn brown. They cover the earth as they fall, creating good hiding places for mice and insects. Trees develop buds for next spring's foliage.

Many crops are ready to be harvested. Gardeners gather their tomatoes, cucumbers, and other vegetables for today's eating and for canning, to eat later. Apples are picked, and cold-weather vegetables like cabbage and radishes are planted.

ANT TRACKING

How Do Ants Respond to Cookie Crumbs?

MATERIALS

ants
cookies

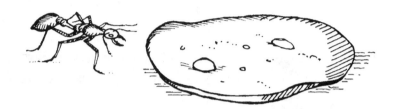

PROCEDURE

1. Find an outside area where there are ants.
2. Crumble the cookies into small crumbs. How do the ants react to the crumbs? How do the ants react to one another?
3. Watch the ants to see where they carry the crumbs.

EXPLANATION

Ants like the sweetness of the cookie crumbs and take them home to their anthills to share with the rest of the ants. Ants have a very elaborate social structure. When one ant finds a food source like a cookie, it leaves a trail for the other ants that tells them where to find the food. Ants do not fight over the cookie crumbs. Instead, they cooperate so that all the ants have food. Ants are also very strong for their size. An ant can carry a crumb that is three times its body size.

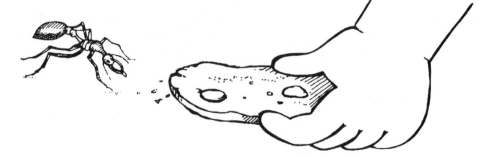

AUTUMN ANTS

Do Ants Know the Difference Between Artificial Sweeteners and Sugar?

MATERIALS

1 teaspoon (5 ml) sugar
tap water
2 cups
package of artificial sweetener
2 bottle caps
ants

PROCEDURE

1. Mix the sugar with a little tap water in one of the cups.
2. Mix the artificial sweetener with the same amount of water used in step 1 in the second cup.
3. Fill one of the bottle caps with the sugar water and the second with the artificial sweetener mixture. Be sure to remember which solution is the sugar and which is the sweetener.
4. Place the caps near the ants. What sweetener do the ants go toward?

EXPLANATION

Ants know the difference between artificial sweetener and real sugar. They went directly to the real sugar because it contains the natural compounds that they eat. Artificial sweeteners contain chemical compounds that are developed in laboratories.

SUGAR WATER

ARTIFICIAL SWEETENER

CAMOUFLAGE NATURALLY

What Is Camouflage in Nature?

MATERIALS

1 sheet each of brown paper, green paper, red
    paper, white paper, and yellow paper
leaves that have fallen

PROCEDURE

1. Fold all the sheets of paper in half.
2. Tear each sheet on the fold. Now you have two
   sheets of paper in each color, or two sets of all the colors.
3. Place the first set of colored sheets in areas where the colors closely match
   the colors of the leaves that have fallen.
4. Place the second set of colored sheets where the colors are very different
   from the colors in the environment.
5. Walk away so you are at a distance from both sets of colored sheets. What
   do you see?

EXPLANATION

Camouflage is the coloring or shading some animals have the disguises them,
or makes them difficult to see in their environment. Camouflage helps animals
hide from their enemies. For example, the swallow butterfly's wings are shades
of green that closely match the leaves of some bushes in its natural environment. The shadow patterns on the coat of a fawn blend in with the animal's
forest habitat. Some animals can change colors depending on their environment. The coats of some types of rabbits change from brown in the summer to
white in the winter to look like snow. In your experiment, you saw that it was
difficult to recognize from a distance the sheets of paper that blended in with
the colors of the environment, demonstrating camouflage.

CARROT TOPS

Why Is the Top of the Carrot Root Green?

MATERIALS

carrots with leaves
magnifying lens

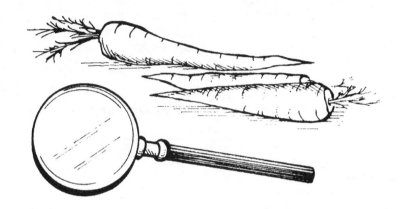

PROCEDURE

1. Look at the carrots carefully.
2. Under the magnifying lens, examine the tops of the carrot roots just below the leaves. What color are they?

EXPLANATION

Almost any plant that is exposed to light turns green. This green is the chlorophyll, which assists in the photosynthesis process. (See "Chlorophyll Test," page 36.) Some of the top portion of the carrot roots you looked at might have been green. This part was green because the top portion of the root was exposed to the sun.

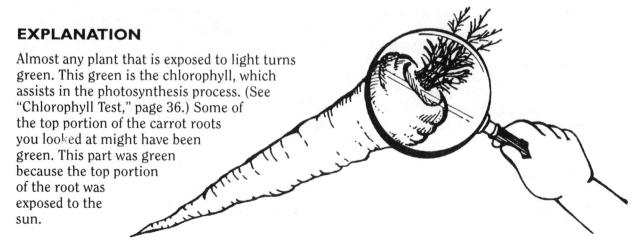

CHERRY SOAK

What Happens to a Cherry When It Is Soaked in Water?

MATERIALS

cup
tap water
ripe cherry

PROCEDURE

1. Fill the cup with tap water.
2. Place the cherry in the cup and let it soak. What happens to the cherry after it has soaked for 5 minutes?

EXPLANATION

When you soaked the cherry in the water, the skin split. This happened because the cherry skin contains tiny holes that let water in, but do not let much water out. Normally, this system is good for the cherry because it reserves the water close to the seed even when it is dry outside. But when you add a lot of water, more water goes inside the cherry than can get out through the holes. The pressure inside the cherry builds up, causing the inside of the cherry to burst its skin.

CRANBERRY DROP

How Are Cranberries Tested for Freshness?

MATERIALS

package of whole cranberries
yardstick (meterstick)

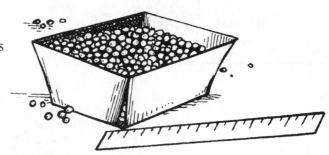

PROCEDURE

1. Select one cranberry at a time.
2. Hold the berry about 7 inches (18 cm) from a wood or tile floor.
3. Drop the berry and watch it bounce.
4. Test the other berries to see whether they all bounce to about the same height.

EXPLANATION

Cranberries are hard, sour berries that grow in marshes and bogs and ripen in the autumn. After harvesting, batches of the berries are selected for testing. The berries are dropped from a height of about 7 inches (18 cm) to determine if they are fresh enough to be shipped to market. Berries that do not bounce are not fresh and are discarded.

DANDELION ELASTIC

How Can You Make a Natural Elastic Material?

MATERIALS

dandelion plant

PROCEDURE

1. Break the stem of the dandelion plant.
2. Squeeze the sap from the stem and use it to coat the end of your finger up to your first knuckle.
3. Let the sap dry for a few minutes.
4. Gently roll the dry, rubbery sap off your finger as you would roll a sock off your foot.
5. Pull the sap in different directions. What happens to the sap?

EXPLANATION

Sap is a juice that flows through plants, carrying food and water to all plant parts. The dandelion sap dried to form an elastic material. When it dried, it became stretchable, like a rubber band.

FRUIT NUTS

What Is the Fruit in Nuts?

MATERIALS

different types of nuts (pistachios, walnuts,
   sweet chestnuts, hazelnuts,
   and brazil nuts, for example)
nutcracker

PROCEDURE

1. Examine the nuts carefully and compare their shells.
2. Crack open the nuts.
3. Examine the insides of the nuts. How do the nuts compare?

EXPLANATION

Nuts are actually fruits that have hard wooden shells. The seeds are called **kernels,** which are the parts of the nut that you eat. Nuts grow in many different shapes and sizes. The coconut is a very large nut. The sapucia nut has a shell that is soft like cork. The pine nut can be eaten with its shell on. Try planting one of your nuts and seeing what grows.

FRUIT SEEDS

How Do the Seeds of Fruits Compare?

MATERIALS

apple
banana
orange
peach
watermelon
knife
adult helper

PROCEDURE

1. Ask an adult helper to cut each of the fruits in half, exposing the seeds.
2. Examine the seeds and their locations. How are the seeds and the fruits alike and different?

EXPLANATION

The banana seeds are the tiniest seeds, whereas the peach seed, or pit, is the largest seed. Watermelons have fairly small seeds for the size of the fruit. Apple seeds are slightly smaller than watermelon seeds. Apples have several seeds; the peach has only one. It is difficult to determine whether the watermelon or the banana has more seeds because banana seeds are so small that they are difficult to count. Banana seeds extend along the length of the banana, just as the seeds in the water-melon fill the fruit. The seeds of oranges, apples, and peaches grow in the center of the fruits.

HIDDEN SEEDS

Where Are the Seeds in Pinecones?

WHITE SPRUCE

BALSAM FIR

MATERIALS

different varieties of pinecones
magnifying lens

PROCEDURE

1. Examine each pinecone from the outside. Are they different colors?
2. Pull one petal off each of the varieties of pinecones. Examine each petal under the magnifying lens.
3. Take each pinecone apart and examine its core (the stalk the petals grow from). How many different parts of the pinecones did you find?

EXPLANATION

Conifers are trees that do not flower. Instead, their seeds develop inside cones. The petals or scales grow from a stalk, just the way branches grow from a tree trunk. Each type of conifer produces a unique cone. Some cones are long, thin, and narrow, whereas others are round and fat. Cones can be tiny or can grow to lengths of more than 12 inches (30 cm). Some cones produce seeds each year; others produce seeds every two years. While the seeds are developing, the scales remain tightly closed. The scales remain closed for several years as the seeds ripen inside. On a warm day, when the cone is ready, it opens and allows the seeds to fly away in the wind.

LEAF DECOMPOSITION

What Happens to a Leaf After It Has Fallen?

MATERIALS

magnifying lens
sheet of white paper

PROCEDURE

1. Check the ground for leaves that have fallen.
2. Under the magnifying lens, inspect several leaves to determine the state of their deterioration.
3. Lay the leaves on the sheet of paper. You may want to arrange the leaves in order from the least to the most deteriorated. Can you detect any causes of the deterioration, such as insect infestation or water damage?

EXPLANATION

Deciduous leaves, from trees that lose their leaves in the winter, blanket the ground, providing food and shelter for many animals. After the leaves have fallen, they go through the process of decomposition, or breaking down. The leaves that have been on the ground the longest are the farthest along in the decomposition process. Animals too tiny to see even under a magnifying lens eat small holes in the leaves. Soon bacteria and **fungi** (plants that need other plants for nourishment, such as mushrooms) begin to break down tougher parts of leaves. Finally, small animals like woodlice and pill bugs eat much of the leaf that remains.

LEAF PIGMENT

What Stages of Color Do Leaves Go Through Before Turning Brown?

MATERIALS

deciduous tree

PROCEDURE

1. Find leaves from a single deciduous tree that have fallen to the ground.
2. Look on the ground and in the tree for leaves of different shades. How many color variations do you find?

EXPLANATION

When leaves change colors, or **pigment,** they do not immediately turn from green to yellow or red or brown. One leaf might go through many different colorations. For example, a tree that turns orange, like the sour gum or mountain ash, goes from green to yellow-green to yellow to yellow-orange to orange to orange-brown to brown. Leaves of these colors can usually be found on the ground around the tree. The leaves of other trees turn beautiful shades of red, like the dogwood and the oak, or yellow like the gingko tree.

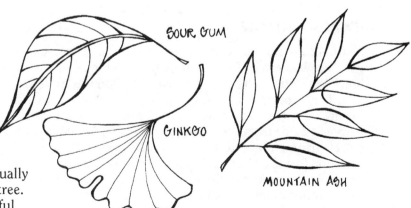

SOUR GUM

GINKGO

MOUNTAIN ASH

LIMESTONE CAVERNS

How Are Stalactites and Stalagmites Formed?

MATERIALS

small seashells
plastic bowl
2 tablespoons (30 ml) white vinegar

PROCEDURE

1. Hold the seashells over the plastic bowl.
2. Pour the white vinegar on the shells and let it drip on the bottom of the bowl.
3. Wait for the puddle in the bottom of the bowl to dry. What do you see?

EXPLANATION

Seashells are made of calcium, which can be dissolved by acids like vinegar. The vinegar dissolved some of the shell material, which could be seen at the bottom of the bowl. When the puddle evaporated, the dissolved material from the shells made a small pile. This process is similar to the way limestone caves are formed in nature. The water from streams dissolves the carbon dioxide from the air to form an acid. As water travels through limestone rocks, it dissolves some of the rock and forms tiny cracks. Water dripping through the cracks in the ceiling of the cave dissolves more limestone. As the water evaporates, the solid limestone remains and deposits slowly, drop by drop, to form **stalactites,** the formations that hang from the tops of caves, and **stalagmites,** which reach up from the floors of caves.

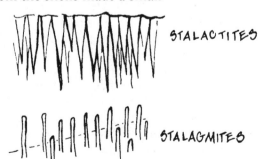

STALACTITES

STALAGMITES

MAKING MOUNTAINS

How Are Mountains Formed?

MATERIALS

modeling clay in three different colors
rolling pin
butter knife
2 wooden blocks

PROCEDURE

1. Roll each color of clay into a strip about 1 inch (2.5 cm) thick.
2. Place the strips on top of one another.
3. Trim the edges with the butter knife so the layers make one strip measuring about 12 inches (30 cm) long by 6 inches (15 cm) wide.
4. Place a wooden block on each short end of the clay strip.
5. Holding each block at the top, slowly push the blocks together at the same time. What happens to the clay?

EXPLANATION

Much of the earth's surface is covered by mountains. They are formed by the movements in the earth's crust when two land masses move toward each other and squeeze the land in between. When you pushed the blocks together, the clay began to buckle. The layers of clay move together in much the same way that the earth shifts. This is why you can sometimes see tilted layers of different kinds of rocks on mountains.

MAPLE FLIGHT

Why Do Maple Tree Seeds Resemble Little Helicopters?

MATERIALS

2 same-sized maple tree seeds

PROCEDURE

1. Keep one of the maple tree seeds intact, but carefully break both wings off the second seed.
2. Hold both seeds in one hand.
3. Stretch your arm as high in the air as you can.
4. Release the two seeds together. Which seed drops to the ground faster?

EXPLANATION

Maple tree seeds look like tiny helicopters. Each seed is attached to two long, papery wings. These wings catch the wind and spin, so the seed falls slowly. The slowly falling seed can be carried by the wind to a place some distance from the parent tree. This is important because it means that the seed may land in a well-lighted area instead of under the shade of the original tree. The more light the tree has, the better its chances for survival. The seed without wings dropped directly to the ground.

MEASURING LICHENS

How Large a Lichen Can You Find?

MATERIALS

lichens
old cemetery
yardstick (meterstick)
magnifying lens

PROCEDURE

1. Search for lichens on old headstones. Lichens look like pale green flaky blotches on rock.
2. Examine the lichens under the magnifying lens.
3. Measure the lichens on each headstone. Find the largest one you can. (*Hint:* You are likely to find the largest ones on the oldest headstones.)

EXPLANATION

Lichens are small plants that attach themselves to objects. They are unusual plants without roots, leaves, or flowers. Lichens need very little food or water. They can live for many years and grow very slowly. Lichens can be found in many different places.

MINT ANTS

How Do Animals React to Certain Scents?

MATERIALS

ants
mint leaves (obtain at a
greenhouse or garden store)

PROCEDURE

1. Find an outdoor area where there are ants.
2. Lay the mint leaves in a circle around the ants. What do the ants do?
3. Remove the mint.
4. Research and experiment with other insects and their reactions to certain plants. How do other insects react to the plants you used?

EXPLANATION

Ants do not like the smell of mint, so they stayed within the area outlined by the mint leaves until you removed the leaves.

Gardeners sometimes use plants and **herbs** to keep insects away. For example, many gardeners plant marigolds to prevent insects from eating their crops. **Aphids** (tiny insects that eat many plants) are kept away by rubbing garlic on plants. Placing bay leaves in a flour canister in the kitchen will prevent the invasion of some insects.

MUSHROOM INSPECTION

What Are Mushrooms?

MATERIALS

mushroom from the grocery store
magnifying lens

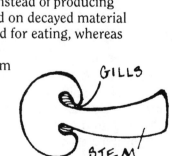

PROCEDURE

1. Inspect the mushroom. What shape is it?
2. Examine the mushroom under the magnifying lens.
3. Notice the very thin layers of skin on the top.
4. Pull part of the skin off. What is under the layer of skin? Is the area below the skin the same color as the part you removed?
5. Notice how the top of the mushroom is attached to the stem.
6. Inspect the fibers and the tiny pores in the top from a side view.
7. Inspect the tiny folds under the top. What purpose do you think they have?

EXPLANATION

Mushrooms grow almost anywhere it is warm and damp enough. They are fungi that do not contain chlorophyll, so they are not green. Instead of producing their own food through photosynthesis, mushrooms feed on decayed material in the soil or on other plants. Some mushrooms are good for eating, whereas others are deadly poisonous. When you inspected the mushroom, you found several parts. When the mushroom is closed, the top may resemble a button. After the top opens, it looks like a tiny umbrella, called the **crown.** A ring attaches the top to the stem. The ridges under the crown are thin growths called **gills.** This area contains millions of spores, which look like powder and which spread to form other mushrooms.

83

NEST INSPECTION

What Do Birds Use to Build Their Nests?

MATERIALS

bird's nest
sheet of white paper
rubber gloves
magnifying lens

PROCEDURE

1. Collect a bird's nest. Before you remove the nest, make sure birds are no longer using it.

2. Lay the sheet of white paper on your work surface and put the gloves on.

3. Lay the nest on the sheet.

4. Gently and carefully pull the nest apart.

5. Examine the pieces of materials under the magnifying lens. What did the bird use to build its nest?

6. Throw away the pieces of nest and discard the rubber gloves.

EXPLANATION

Birds' nests should never be touched in the spring or summer or when birds are still living in them. Birds use a variety of materials to build their nests, and different types of birds build different types of nests. Robins' nests always include a cradle of mud and grass. These cradles hang below the branch. The mourning dove builds a nest of twigs so thin that the eggs can be seen through it. The ruby-throated hummingbird makes a cup-shaped nest out of soft materials, including cobwebs and pieces of plants. The outside might be decorated with lichens and insect cocoons. Other birds build nests with other types of materials.

QUICK SPOIL

Why Do Some Foods Spoil Quickly?

MATERIALS

apple

PROCEDURE

1. Take a bite out of the apple.
2. Let the apple stand for a few minutes. What happens?

EXPLANATION

Fruits and vegetables are protected by their skins or peels. When you took a bite out of the apple, you removed the skin that was protecting the inside. The inside was exposed to the air, and an oxidation process began. **Oxidation** is a chemical reaction that causes the inside of the apple to react with the oxygen and begin to decay.

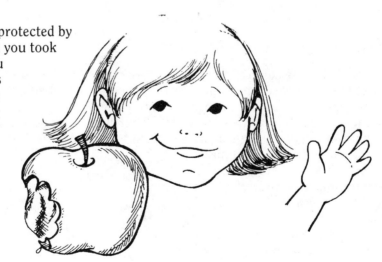

ROCK COLLECTION

How Are Rocks Alike and Different?

MATERIALS

collection of rocks from different areas
magnifying lens
field guide to rocks

PROCEDURE

1. Examine each of the rocks under the magnifying lens.
2. Use the field guide to identify each type of rock according to its distinguishing characteristics. How are the rocks alike and different?

EXPLANATION

Rocks are solids that are composed of one or more minerals. They are classified according to how they are formed. **Igneous** rocks are formed when hot, molten magma flows out of the earth and cools. Peridotite is an example of an igneous rock. **Sedimentary** rocks are created when small particles, such as the sand and silt at the bottom of a pond, settle and are pressed together by the weight of the materials above them. Sandstone is an example of a sedimentary rock. **Metamorphic** rocks are rocks that have undergone a change because of extreme heat and pressure. Slate is an example of a metamorphic rock.

peridotite IGNEOUS

sandstone

SEDIMENTARY

slate

METAMORPHIC

ROCK SMOOTHING

Why Are Rocks in Streams and Rivers Smooth?

MATERIALS

several tiny pieces of brick
plastic jar with a screw-on lid
tap water
2 or 3 helpers

PROCEDURE

1. Closely examine the edges of the pieces of brick.
2. Place several pieces in the plastic jar.
3. Fill the jar with tap water and screw the lid on so it is tight.
4. Taking turns with friends and family members, each person should shake the jar about 100 times.
5. Open the jar. What do you notice about the pieces of brick?

EXPLANATION

The brick pieces have smoother surfaces than they did when you placed them in the jar. The swirling action of the water wore away their sharp edges. The constant movement of water in streams, rivers, and oceans causes rocks to become smooth.

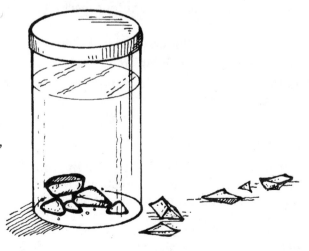

ROTTING TREE

What Can Be Found in a Rotting Tree Trunk?

MATERIALS

rotting tree
plastic gloves
trowel
tweezers
jar
magnifying lens

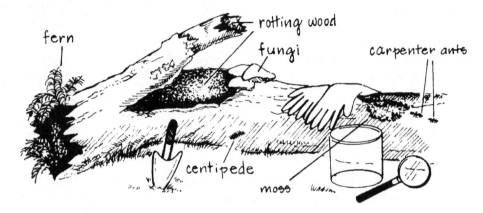

PROCEDURE

1. Find a rotting tree in a wooded area.
2. Put on the plastic gloves.
3. Use the trowel to move and uncover materials on the tree.
4. Use the tweezers to collect items you want to inspect further and put these in the jar.
5. Look for signs of rotting wood. Rotten wood looks like a brown dust.
6. Use the magnifying lens to look for fungi and insects.
7. Examine the rotting wood to see if ferns or moss are growing on it. What types of insects are in the wood?

EXPLANATION

Dead trees are recycled, or used again in a different form, by nature. Wormlike beetle larvae eat through some of the bark. Insects and bacteria change the wood into a soft, moist substance that provides a good growing place for moss, ferns, and fungi. Millipedes, centipedes, bark beetles, carpenter ants, and termites might be eating the rotting wood of your tree. All of these creatures help turn the rotting tree into soil that will soon be able to nourish a new tree.

SEEDS GALORE

What Is a Compound Flower?

MATERIALS

dandelion flower
magnifying lens
scissors

PROCEDURE

1. Pick a dandelion flower.
2. Examine the flower under the magnifying lens.
3. Look carefully at all of the petals.
4. Cut the flower in half and examine the inside closely. What do you see?
5. Look for a dandelion that has turned into a puffball of seeds.
6. Examine the seeds, then blow on them to see how they fly through the wind.

EXPLANATION

The dandelion begins blooming in the spring and lasts well into the autumn. It belongs to a family called **compound flowers** because their flowers are composed of tiny clusters, or **florets.** Each floret consists of a band of thin petals that have grown together to form one flower. Each thin petal has the capability of producing one seed, which is why dandelion plants spread so quickly. When you looked at the flower that you cut in half, you saw hundreds of petals attached to the sepal of the plant. The petals turn into feathery stalks, each with a seed attached. When you blow on the puffy dandelion, the seeds float through the air, and other dandelions will begin to grow where they land.

FLORETS

STEM

STAR PATTERN

How Can You Make Your Own Constellation?

MATERIALS

oatmeal box
pencil
large needle
flashlight small enough to fit
    in the oatmeal box
guide to constellations

PROCEDURE

1. On the bottom of the oatmeal box, draw dots in a pattern that stars make in the sky. Copy a constellation pattern.
2. With the needle, poke holes in the dots you have made.
3. Darken the room.
4. Turn the flashlight on and aim the beam at the bottom of the box.
5. Point the bottom of the box toward the ceiling. What do you see when you turn the flashlight on?

EXPLANATION

Constellations are clusters of stars that people have seen as patterns. When you poked holes in the bottom of the box, you created a star pattern. The light passing through the holes projected this pattern on the ceiling. This is similar to the way the image of stars is projected in a planetarium.

TREE DAMAGE

How Does a Tree Heal Itself?

MATERIALS

trees
magnifying lens

PROCEDURE

1. Examine several trees for signs of damage.
2. When you find a damaged tree, study the wound under the magnifying lens. How do you think the tree was wounded? What kinds of signs show that the tree healed itself?

EXPLANATION

Weather conditions, fires, people, and animals all wound trees. When a tree is damaged, it first leaks sap from the wound opening. In most cases, a callus quickly forms at the edges. This keeps the sap from oozing out. Cells in the **cambium,** or growth tissue, begin to multiply and grow inward. If the edges are jagged, the opening may never close completely. Large wounds form permanent scars on the surface. You can see these as knots in the tree's bark.

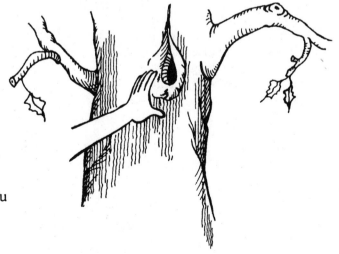

TREE STUMP

What Can a Tree Stump Tell You?

MATERIALS

tree stumps

PROCEDURE

1. Find several different tree stumps.
2. Examine the stumps for rings and holes. Can you tell why the tree had to be cut down? Can you tell how old the tree was when it was cut down? Compare several tree stumps.

EXPLANATION

If the tree had a hole in the center of the stump, it might have been cut down because it was infested with insects. By counting the rings of the tree you can tell the approximate age of the tree when it was cut down. The rings in the early years of the tree's life are usually wider because growth is more rapid in these years.

WATER SPEED

How Can the Velocity of Water Be Determined?

MATERIALS

ribbon
stream
floating object
stopwatch

Ping pong ball

PROCEDURE

1. Place the ribbon on a tree or bush next to the stream.
   This ribbon will designate the finishing point of your activity.

2. Walk about 1 yard (1 m) upstream from the ribbon.

3. Drop the floating object in the stream and click on the stopwatch at the same time.

4. When the object reaches the ribbon, click off the stopwatch.

5. To determine the speed of the moving water, divide the distance the object floated, which was about 1 yard (1 m), by the number of minutes or seconds it took the object to reach the ribbon.

EXPLANATION

Velocity is the speed of water. The water's velocity affects the oxygen content of the water. The faster the water moves, the higher the oxygen content will be. Oxygen content is a major factor that determines what types of plants and animals live in a stream.

WINTER

 Winter is a time of rest and dormancy for many living things. Freezing temperatures, thickening ice, and blowing snow are characteristics of winter in the northernmost parts of the country. Frost makes designs on the edges of windowpanes. The sky is often dark and dreary, except for the glory of the snow as it falls.

Tracks in the snow mark the movements of animals. Squirrels and other animals have thick coats or fur. Bears sleep through the winter, and chipmunks stay inside their holes. Birds fluff out their feathers and pull their necks in on cold days. Many have migrated to warmer climates as others seek food supplies through the snow and on brittle plants.

Frogs, turtles, and snakes hide underground. Some sleep deep beneath the snow. Others hibernate in mud at the bottom of ponds. Black dots can be found in snowshoe tracks. These are snowfleas, one of the true insects of winter.

Plants struggle to survive the winter. They shrivel up in an effort to stay warm, their juices buried deep within their roots. Some plants maintain a little water deep inside their cells, avoiding the freeze. Trees without leaves have stopped growing. Conifers keep their leaves and store water in their waxy needles. Grass is brown and dry.

No matter how cold, still, and dark the winter may seem, the many and varied life forms that populate the earth are not dead but merely resting and preparing for the vigorous new spring season when the cycle will begin again.

BARK INVESTIGATION

How Does the Bark of Trees Differ?

MATERIALS

several trees
magnifying lens
2 sheets of paper
pencil

PROCEDURE

1. Examine the bark of the different trees under the magnifying lens. Look for trees with different textures, colors, and interesting characteristics.

2. On one of the sheets of paper, note the characteristics of the bark you find.

3. Try holding the second sheet against the bark and rubbing the smooth side of your pencil lead against the paper.

EXPLANATION

The bark is the outer wood of the tree trunk and branches. It protects the tree and helps keep water inside. Bark is a dead layer of the tree that cannot grow. As the tree grows, the bark cracks and falls off. Each tree has a unique pattern of cracks and ridges. Some trees, like the white birch, shed a thin layer of bark each year. Cork trees have heavy-textured, soft bark with large pores. Crepe myrtle has bark that peels naturally. The mountain ash has smooth, dark gray bark. What other kinds of bark can you find?

BLOWING SNOW

How Does the Wind Blow Snow?

MATERIALS

recent snowfall

PROCEDURE

1. Go outdoors after a snowfall.
2. Look at the trees and the surface of the snow. Which direction did the snow come from?

EXPLANATION

Snow usually sticks to the sides of trees. The snowy sides of a row of trees will show you which way the wind was blowing during the last snowfall—from the snowy side. When the wind blows over a lightweight snow, it causes the snow to pile in drifts. The sloping side of the drift faces the direction from which the wind blew.

BLUBBER INSULATION

What Keeps a Seal from Freezing in Icy Water?

MATERIALS

large spoon
solid vegetable shortening
2 large plastic zip bags
cold tap water
bag of ice
pail

OPEN BAG

CLOSED BAG WITH SHORTENING

PROCEDURE

1. Spoon the vegetable shortening into one
   of the plastic bags until the bag is about half full.
2. Release most of the air from the bag and zip the bag closed.
3. Slip this bag into the second bag, but do not zip the second bag closed.
4. Set the plastic bags aside.
5. Pour cold tap water and ice into the pail so it is about half full.
6. Slip the open bag on your hand and mold the shortening around to cover all
   of your hand. Be sure not to open the bag that is closed.
7. Place both hands in the icy water for about 20 seconds. How do your hands feel?

EXPLANATION

The hand covered with the shortening did not become cold, but the bare hand did.
Seals and sea lions are mammals, which means they are warm-blooded. Many of
them live in very cold waters. They have a thick layer of **blubber,** or fat, under the
skin to protect them from the icy water. When you covered your hand with the
shortening, you surrounded your hand with a fatty substance that resembles
blubber. When you put this hand into the cold water, it took a long time to feel
the cold because the shortening insulated your hand.

BUD ANALYSIS

What Does a Branch of Buds Indicate About a Tree?

MATERIALS

trees
magnifying lens
field guide to trees

PROCEDURE

1. Walk through an outdoor area and find a tree with buds on it.
2. Look at the end of the branch under the magnifying lens.
3. Find the part of the branch that has two different colors and a scale or ring around it.
4. Look for other scales around the branch.
5. Notice the arrangements of the buds. Are some buds situated directly across from one another or do they alternate on the branch? Does the branch have clusters of buds all at the end or are the buds spread out? Are the buds covered with a furlike substance or are they clean? Are the buds compacted or are they open like tiny leaves?
6. Use the field guide to identify the types of trees you examined.

EXPLANATION

Winter buds contain materials the plant needs to grow quickly when spring arrives. When you look at the rings, or **scales,** that separate two different colors at the end of a branch, you can see how much that branch grew during the year. Bud scales preserve water and protect the delicate tissues inside. Trees can be identified easily by the arrangement and shape of their buds.

SCALE (NEW GROWTH)

MAGNOLIA

BUD

99

COLD HANDS

Why Is It Difficult to Pick Up Objects When Your Hands Are Cold?

MATERIALS

coins
pushpins
plastic zip bag
ice cubes
timer

PROCEDURE

1. Place some coins and pushpins on a table and practice picking them up and putting them back down. Notice how easy this is to do.

2. Fill the plastic bag with ice cubes and zip the bag closed.

3. Hold the bag in one hand for about 2 minutes. It will be difficult, but you can do it!

4. Put the bag down on the table.

5. Try to pick up the pushpins and coins with your cold hand. How easy is this to do now?

EXPLANATION

Beneath the skin of your hands are sensitive **nerve endings.** These nerve endings relay what your hands feel to your brain. When it is cold, the nerve endings become numb and less sensitive, making it difficult for you to do simple tasks like picking up objects. It was much easier to pick up the coins and pushpins before you held the bag of ice cubes.

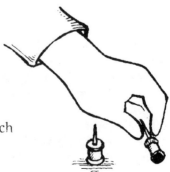

CRYSTAL STUDY

How Do Snowflakes Differ?

MATERIALS

snowflakes
sheet of black paper
magnifying lens

PROCEDURE

1. During a snowfall, catch some snowflakes on the sheet of black paper.
2. Study each snowflake under the magnifying lens. How are the snowflakes alike and different?

EXPLANATION

Each snowflake is a collection of ice crystals. **Ice crystals** are made of water vapor that has frozen. It is hard to find two snowflakes that look alike because the crystals all grow slightly differently. They might be shaped like needles, hexagons, columns, plates, or prisms. Their shape depends upon the temperature, height, and water content of the cloud in which they formed.

EVERGREEN LEAVES

Why Don't Evergreens Lose Their Leaves?

MATERIALS

evergreen tree
magnifying lens

PROCEDURE

1. Examine the needles of
   an evergreen tree under the magnifying lens.
2. With your fingernail, scrape off some of the
   substance that covers one of the needles. How does it feel?
3. Break open one of the needles. Look at the inside under the
   magnifying lens. What do you see?

EXPLANATION

Evergreens do not lose their leaves in the winter as
deciduous trees do. Most evergreens have needlelike
leaves that can withstand the cold. Their pores close off
to protect the inside of the plant. The outside of each
needle is coated with a waxy layer that protects the needle
from frost damage. Inside each needle is a sticky liquid the tree uses for
nourishment during the winter. Eventually these needles become old and
damaged and will shed.

FROST FORMATION

How Does Frost Form?

MATERIALS

20 ice cubes
tin can
1 teaspoon (5 ml) salt
spoon

PROCEDURE

1. Place the ice cubes in the tin can.
2. Add the salt and mix rapidly.
3. Watch the frost form on the outside of the can.

EXPLANATION

Frost is formed when air containing moisture in the
form of water is cooled below freezing temperature.
The moisture condenses and collects as frost on cold
surfaces. Frost usually forms on clear nights. Farmers
pay particular attention to the sky on chilly nights,
looking for a cloudless sky, which means a killing frost.
Low temperatures cause plant juices to freeze and
swell, bursting delicate plant cells. By placing the ice
cubes in the can, you caused the can to become very
cold. The salt causes the ice to melt. Tiny droplets
of water in the air immediately attached themselves
to the sides of the can and froze there.

GARDEN PLAN

What Type of Garden Can You Grow?

MATERIALS

seed and plant catalogs
yardstick (meterstick)
pencil
sheet of notebook paper

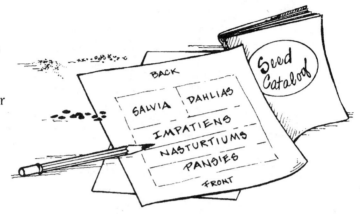

PROCEDURE

1. Look through the catalogs to find interesting plants for your summer garden. Read about the plants and pay careful attention to the information given about temperature zones. Be sure to select plants that can grow in your zone.

2. Ask your parents to set aside a space outside that you can use for your garden. Measure the space to help you determine how many plants will fit into it.

3. Plan your garden on paper by sketching a garden you would like to plant and labeling it. Think about how tall the plants you have chosen will grow. Plan to put tall flowers in the back and smaller flowers in the front.

4. Order the seeds you need and get ready for spring!

EXPLANATION

Gardeners often plan their summer flower gardens during the winter. Many people receive seed and plant catalogs in the mail, and these are excellent planning guides. Each catalog includes information on the temperature a plant needs, how much light it must have, what kind of soil is best for it, how big it grows, and so on. Use all of this information when planning your garden.

GLACIER SCRAPE

How Do Glaciers Change the Environment?

MATERIALS

ice cube
cup of sand
small board of soft wood (pine)

PROCEDURE

1. Place the ice cube on the sand for a minute until some of the sand sticks to the ice.
2. Rub the sandy side of the cube on the board for a few seconds.
3. Place the cube in the sand again just long enough to pick up additional sand.
4. Again, rub the sandy side of the cube on the board for a few seconds.
5. Repeat this procedure about ten times.
6. Let the board stand for a few minutes.
7. Examine the surface of the board. What do you see?

EXPLANATION

Glaciers are masses of ice that flow through mountain valleys, creeping down as they melt. As they move, glaciers collect rock fragments, which may be large boulders, tiny sand particles, or anything in between. Picking up these rock fragments is called **entraining.** The glacier and the rock fragments scrape across the surface of the earth, wearing it away and leaving gorges and other land forms. When you scraped the ice cube on the soft wood, you scraped some of the wood away. You might also have seen bits of sand stuck to the surface of the board, just as glaciers leave rocks behind when they move down a mountain.

HEATING HANDS

Why Does Rubbing Your Hands Together Make Them Warmer?

MATERIALS

your hands

PROCEDURE

1. Go outside on a cold day without gloves on.
2. Rub your hands together rapidly.

EXPLANATION

Heat is the energy given off by moving **molecules,** or tiny elements, and atoms. When you rubbed your hands together, you caused the molecules in your hands to move faster. The increased movement of the molecules caused heat to be released, so your hands became warmer for a few seconds.

ICE MELT

Why Do Road Crews Use Salt on Icy Roads?

MATERIALS

2 ice cubes
½ teaspoon (2.5 ml) salt
2 cups

PROCEDURE

1. Place one ice cube in each cup.
2. Shake the salt onto one of the cubes. What happens after a few minutes?

EXPLANATION

The ice cube with the salt on it melted faster than the other ice cube. Salt helps lower the melting point of ice because salt will not freeze until the temperature reaches –22° F (–30° C). In winter, road crews spread salt on roads to help melt the ice and snow.

ICE SPACE

Does Ice Occupy More Space Than Water?

MATERIALS

ice cube
small plastic cup
tap water

PROCEDURE

1. Place the ice cube in the cup.
2. Pour tap water into the cup up to the rim.
3. Place the cup in a warm area and wait for several minutes until most of the ice has melted. What do you notice about the water level in the cup?

EXPLANATION

The water level in the cup dropped. The water went down because when the ice melted, the water that took its place occupied less space than the ice cube. When water is frozen, it forms crystals with air spaces between them. This is why ice occupies more space than water. It is also why you hear cracking and popping noises when you put ice cubes into liquid. As the ice melts, air is released.

OUTSIDE BREATH

Why Can You See Your Breath on Cold Days?

MATERIALS

cold morning

PROCEDURE

Go outside on a cold morning and blow in the air. What do you see?

EXPLANATION

Your lungs are warm, so when you breathe out, your lungs push out warm, moist air. The cold air outside cannot hold as much moisture as warm air, so the moisture in your breath condenses into tiny droplets as it becomes cooler. You can see these tiny droplets floating in the air.

POND MELT

What Collects in the Ice of a Frozen Pond?

MATERIALS

plastic bowl
magnifying lens
*You must have access to a
    partially frozen pond.*

PROCEDURE

1. Collect a few pieces of ice from the edges of the pond. *Caution: Do not go
    out on the pond to get the ice. Collect it as you stand on the shore.*
2. Place the ice in the plastic bowl and go inside.
3. Let the ice melt at room temperature and examine the water under the
    magnifying lens. What do you see in the pond water?

EXPLANATION

When the pond freezes, small insects, as well as other debris,
are captured in the ice. Close
inspection of the water will
reveal different types of
materials such as
leaves, twigs, and
organisms, that
were floating on
the pond when it
froze.

TWIG

SEED HEADS

GRASS

MOSS

WORM

INSECT

SILENT SNOW

Why Does Sound Seem Muffled During a Snowfall?

MATERIALS

snowfall

PROCEDURE

1. Go outside during a snowfall.
2. Listen to the sounds around you.

EXPLANATION

Snowflakes are light and airy crystals with millions of tiny spaces between them. The spaces can absorb sounds. These crystals cause the sounds in the environment to be somewhat muffled—like what you might hear with your head under a pillow.

SILLY SENSES

How Can Your Sense of Touch Be Tricked?

MATERIALS

3 plastic bowls
very warm (almost hot) tap water
ice water
tap water at room temperature

VERY WARM ROOM TEMPERATURE ICY

PROCEDURE

1. Fill one of the bowls with very warm tap water.
2. Fill the second bowl with ice water.
3. Fill the third bowl with tap water at room temperature.
4. Arrange the bowls so the one containing the water at room temperature is in the middle.
5. Place one hand in the very warm water and the other in the ice water for about 1 minute.
6. Then place both hands in the water at room temperature. What do you feel in each hand?

EXPLANATION

The hand that was in the ice water felt hot in the water that was at room temperature. The hand that was in the very warm water felt cold in the room temperature water. This experience is known as **sensory adaptation.** Your senses were trying to figure out what to feel. When the senses are exposed to a strong sensation for a while, they can be fooled when they are quickly exposed to another sensation. Your sense receptors need time to get used to the change.

SINKING SHOES

Why Do Skis Stay on Top of the Snow?

MATERIALS

snow boots
snow
skis

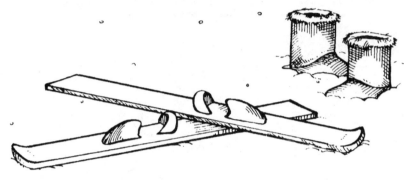

PROCEDURE

1. Put on the snow boots and walk in the snow.
2. Try different ways to stay on top of the snow.
3. Put on the skis. What happens when you move in the snow with skis on?

EXPLANATION

When you walked in the snow wearing your boots, you sank in. When you put on skis, you glided on top of the snow. When you wore the snow boots, your weight was concentrated in a small area. The force per unit area, or pressure, is high enough to penetrate the surface of the snow. When you put on skis, your weight was distributed over a larger area. This decreased the pressure, so you did not sink into the snow.

SNOW PACK

What Is the Difference Between Packed and Unpacked Snow?

MATERIALS

2 cups
snow
2 measuring cups

UNPACKED SNOW   PACKED SNOW

PROCEDURE

1. Fill one cup with unpacked snow and the other with packed snow.
2. Place the cups near a heat source and let the snow melt.
3. Pour the water left in each cup into a separate measuring cup. Which cup held more water?

EXPLANATION

The cup of packed snow contained more water than the cup of unpacked snow. When you packed the snow down in the cup, you pushed the snow crystals closer together. This process eliminated much of the air space between the snow crystals and allowed you to put more snow in the cup. Ten inches (25 cm) of average unpacked snow is about equal to 1 inch (2.5 cm) of water. Heavy or wet snow has a higher water content. Four to 5 inches (10 to 12.5 cm) of wet snow may contain 1 inch (2.5 cm) of water. A dry, powdery snow might require 15 inches (37.5 cm) of snow to equal 1 inch (2.5 cm) of water.

UNPACKED SNOW WATER

PACKED SNOW WATER

114

SNOW TRACKS

What Animal Tracks Can You Find in the Snow?

MATERIALS

fresh snowfall
field guide to animal tracks

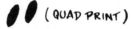(ALTERNATING STEP PATTERN)

 deer  porcupine 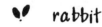 (QUAD PRINT) rabbit

PROCEDURE

1. After a fresh snowfall, search for animal tracks.
2. Examine the tracks. Use the field guide to identify the animal that made the tracks.
3. Notice the size of the tracks, the distance between the tracks, and whether the tracks come in pairs or alternate.
4. Compare the tracks of different animals.

(DUAL PRINT)
finch

EXPLANATION

Animal tracks are easy to see in fresh snow. You may see tracks left by dogs, squirrels, deer, rabbits, or even raccoons. You might be able to tell whether the animal was moving fast or slow by the distance between the tracks. There are three types of track patterns. The **alternating step pattern** is created when an animal places the hind feet into the holes made by the forefeet. Wolves, beavers, porcupines, cats, and deer make alternating step tracks. Another type of tracks is **dual prints.** These tracks are made when an animal bounces forward with two feet at the same time, leaving footprints in pairs. Squirrels make these types of tracks. **Quad prints** are made when animals such as mice, rabbits, and rats leave four distinct prints as they bounce along. These animals bring their hind legs ahead of their front paws before launching into the next stride.

115

STAR GAZE

How Can You Identify the Constellations?

MATERIALS

guide to constellations

PROCEDURE

1. Look at the guide to constellations and try to memorize some of the constellations and their names.
2. Go outside on a clear, dark night and lie on your back to look at the stars. To begin your constellation hunt, find Polaris, the North Star.
3. See how many constellations you can locate from the North Star.

EXPLANATION

Constellations are patterns of stars. When looking for constellations, it helps to find the North Star, Polaris, first because it is very bright and is visible year round. Polaris is the last star in the handle of the Little Dipper, so if you find Polaris, you can follow the stars up the Little Dipper's handle to its bowl. When you have found the Little Dipper, you should be able to find the Big Dipper nearby.

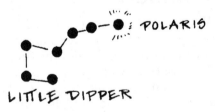

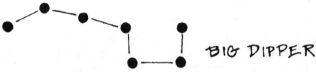

STICKING CUBES

How Can You Make Ice Cubes Stick Together?

MATERIALS

winter gloves
2 ice cubes

PROCEDURE

1. Put on the gloves.
2. Hold one ice cube in each hand and push the cubes together, putting some pressure on each.
3. Watch between the cubes for some of the ice to melt.
4. Release the pressure and hold the ice cubes for a second or two. What happens?

EXPLANATION

When you pressed the ice cubes together, you melted a thin layer on each cube. When you released the pressure, you allowed the water to refreeze, and the ice cubes stuck together. When you ice skate, the pressure of the skates on the ice causes the ice to melt a little, providing a thin, slippery layer of water. After you have skated past that area of ice, the layer of water immediately freezes again.

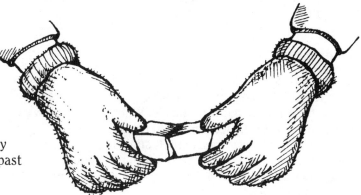

STRINGING ICE

How Can You Make an
Ice Cube Stick to a String?

MATERIALS

ice cube
piece of string about
    6 inches (15 cm) long
salt
timer

PROCEDURE

1. Place the ice cube on a flat surface.
2. Put the string across the top of the ice cube so that half of it extends down each side of the cube.
3. Sprinkle the salt on the cube where the string crosses it.
4. Wait about 3 minutes.
5. Take one end of the string in each hand and lift. What happens to the cube?

EXPLANATION

You were able to pick up the ice cube with the string. Salt makes ice melt because it lowers the melting point of the ice. When you added salt to the ice cube, you caused the area around the string to melt slightly. The string formed a groove in the ice cube. Then, because of the coldness of the ice, the water refroze, encasing the string.

TREE AGE

How Can You Determine the Age of a Pine Tree Without Counting the Rings?

MATERIALS

pine tree

PROCEDURE

1. Look at the branches of the pine tree. Notice the groups of circles of branches around the tree.
2. Count the groups of circles that go completely up the tree to determine the tree's age.

EXPLANATION

It is easy to determine the age of a pine tree without counting the inside rings. Each year a pine tree adds a new circle of branches around its trunk. By counting the circles of branches, you can determine the tree's age. But inspect the trunk carefully to make sure no one has cut off a row of branches.

WARM COVERING

How Cold Is Snow at Different Depths?

MATERIALS

snowbank
2 thermometers

PROCEDURE

1. Stick one of the thermometers well into the top of the snowbank.
2. Stick the second thermometer well into the bottom of the snowbank.
3. Let the thermometers stay in the snow for about 10 minutes. What do the thermometer readings indicate?

EXPLANATION

When you read the thermometers, the one in the bottom of the snowbank registered a warmer temperature than the one at the top. Snow acts as a blanket to insulate and warm the ground. Animals burrow into snow to keep warm during the winter.

WINTER BUBBLES

How Does Blowing Bubbles in Winter Affect the Bubbles?

MATERIALS

1 cup (250 ml) dishwashing liquid
2 cups (500 ml) warm tap water
plastic bowl
4 tablespoons (60 ml) glycerine
1 teaspoon (5 ml) sugar
bubble blower

PROCEDURE

1. Mix the dishwashing liquid and the warm tap water in the plastic bowl.
2. Add the glycerine.
3. Add the sugar.
4. Go outside on a cold night and blow bubbles with the solution. What do you notice about the bubbles?
5. Blow bubbles inside and compare these with the ones you blew outside.

EXPLANATION

Water and dishwashing liquid form a thin film that can be inflated with air to form a bubble. Soap bubbles are shaped by the balance between the outward pressure of the gas inside them and the force of surface tension holding the liquid of the bubbles together. **Surface tension** is the force of the molecules in water attracting one another. Sometimes the bubbles appear to be motionless. If it is cold enough, the bubbles will sparkle as they freeze, and if they hit the snow, they will bounce.

WINTER WARMTH

Which Natural Fibers Keep You the Warmest?

MATERIALS

6-inch (15-cm) piece each of silk, wool,
    and cotton fabric
3 ice cubes
3 rubber bands

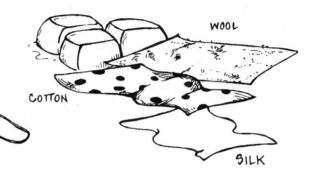

STEPS

1. Wrap each of the pieces of fabric around an ice cube. Keep each piece in place with a rubber band.

2. Set the wrapped cubes in the sun for a few minutes.

3. Unwrap and examine the ice cubes. Which fabrics allow the ice to melt the most and the least?

EXPLANATION

Some clothing is made from natural fibers and threads from animals and plants. Fabrics made from natural fibers help keep people warm in the winter by insulating them from the cool air. Cotton is the most widely used plant fiber and is frequently used in summer clothing because it does not hold the heat next to the body. The strongest fabric is silk, which is obtained from silkworms. The most commonly used animal fiber is sheep's wool. Wool is used for winter clothing because it keeps people very warm. The ice cube with the wool wrapped around it should have melted last because wool is an excellent insulator.

WINTER WORLD

Why Does Winter Come to Certain Areas at Certain Times of the Year?

MATERIALS

apple
stick
lamp with shade removed

PROCEDURE

1. Put the apple through the stick at an angle so that the apple tilts as shown in the drawing.
2. In a darkened room, turn on the lamp.
3. Move the tilted apple around the lamp without changing the angle of the tilt. Notice when the light is shining on the stem of the apple.
4. Continue to move the tilted apple around the lamp and watch the top half become shaded. This represents summer in the southern hemisphere and winter in the northern hemisphere.
5. Look at the middle part of the apple. What does this part represent on the earth?

EXPLANATION

Every 24 hours the earth spins around once on an imaginary axis. This axis is represented by your tilted stick. While it is spinning, the earth is also traveling through space in an **orbit** (circular path) around the sun. The complete trip takes one year, which is split into seasons. When one hemisphere is tilted away from the sun, the sun's rays hit the earth at an angle and are therefore not as strong. This creates the winter season. When you looked at the middle part of the apple, it always remained lighted by the lamp. This represents the **equator.** At the equator, the sun's rays are always at the most direct angle, so it is always hot.

123

Nature and Environmental Organizations

Your local library is an excellent source of information about nature. But you may also want to contact some organizations concerned with the earth. They will be able to provide you with a wealth of information

American Forestry Association
1516 P Street NW
Washington, DC 20005
(202)667-3300

American Geological Institute
422 King Street
Alexandria, VA 22302
(703)379-2480

Canadian Museum of Nature
222 Nepean Street
Ottawa, Ontario K1P 6P4
CANADA
(613) 990-6416

Canadian Wildlife Federation
1673 Carling Avenue
Ottawa, Ontario K2A 3Z1
CANADA
(613)721-2286

Care for the Earth
P.O. Box 289
Sacramento, CA 94101

Center for Marine Conservation
1725 DeSales Street NW
Washington, DC 20036
(202)429-5609

The Children's Rainforest
P.O. Box 936
Lewiston, ME 04240

Coastal Conservation Association
4801 Woodway Street
Houston, TX 77036
(713)626-4222

Cousteau Society
870 Greenbrier Avenue
Chesapeake, VA 23320
(804)523-9335

Friends of the Earth
251 Laurier Avenue West
Ottawa, Ontario K1P 5J6
CANADA
(613) 230-3352

Hug the Earth
P.O. Box 621
Wayne, PA 19087

International Wildlife Coalition
70 East Falmouth Highway
Falmouth, MA 02531
(508) 548-8328

National Association of Academies
    of Science
University of South Carolina
Mathematical Sciences
Columbia, SC 29208
(803)777-7007

National Geographic Society
17th and M Streets NW
Washington, DC 20036
(202)857-7000

National Museum of Natural
    Sciences
Victoria Memorial Museum Building
Metcalfe and McLeod Streets
Ottawa, Ontario K1A OM8
CANADA

National Wildlife Federation
1400 16th Street NW
Washington, DC 10036
(202)797-6800

New York Zoological Society
185 Street and Southern Boulevard
Bronx, NY 10460
(718)364-4275

Redpath Museum
856 Sherbrooke Street West
Montreal, Quebec H3A 2K6
CANADA
(514)398-4087

Royal Ontario Museum
100 Queen's Park
Toronto, Ontario M5S 2C6
CANADA
(416)586-5549

Saskatchewan Museum of Natural
    History
Wascana Park
College and Albert Streets
Regina, Saskatchewan SP4 3V7
CANADA
(306)787-2815

Western Canada Wilderness
    Committee
20 Water Street
Vancouver, BC V6B 1A4
CANADA
(604)683-8220

World Wildlife Fund Canada
50 St. Clair Avenue East
Toronto, Ontario M5T 1N8
CANADA
(416)489-8800

Glossary

acid rain: very weak acid that collects in rain water from polluted air.

albumen: white part of the egg that holds the yellow part.

alternating step pattern: animal paw prints made by placing the hind feet into the holes made by the forefeet.

aphids: tiny insects that eat many plants.

barbs: tiny, hairlike sections of a feather.

barbule: hairlike branch growing from the barb of a feather.

blubber: fat in some animals that keeps them warm.

buoyancy: ability of an object to stay afloat.

calcium: soft, silvery-white mineral.

cambium: growth tissue in the stems and roots of plants.

camouflage: type of disguise used by nature to enable creatures to blend into backgrounds.

carbon dioxide: gas made up of carbon and oxygen.

chalazea: two spiral bands connecting the yolk to the lining of the egg.

chlorophyll: green pigment in plants that traps sunlight energy for making food.

circuli: fish scales with round, bony ridges.

cirrus clouds: feathery, curly, fast-moving clouds; the highest in the sky.

compound flowers: tiny clusters consisting of a band of thin petals grown together to form one flower.

condense: change the state of a substance from a vapor to a liquid.

conifer: cone-bearing tree.

constellation: clusters of stars in the sky that form patterns.

cotyledon: first single leaf or first pair of leaves produced by the embryo of a plant.

crown: the top of a mushroom.

cumulus clouds: thick collections of puffy heaps or domes that may become thunder clouds.

currents: water in the sea constantly circulating in orderly patterns.

deciduous: plants that lose their leaves during a certain season.

decompose: break down compounds into simpler forms.

dense: having the parts very close together.

dual prints: prints made where animals bounce forward two feet at a time, leaving footprints in pairs.

ecology: study of living things and their relationship to their environment.

ecosystem: an environment for organisms.

embryo: miniature plant inside a seed.

endosperm: food supply inside a seed.

entraining: dragging along.

equator: an imaginary line around the center of the earth equidistant from the north and south poles.

erosion: wearing away of land by the forces of nature.

florets: small flowers, usually parts of a dense cluster.

fossils: preserved forms or parts of animals and plants that lived long ago.

fungi: plants that reproduce by spores without any chlorophyll.

funnel web: outside spider web that looks like a circle of wires.

gills: ridges under the crown of a mushroom.

glacier: mass of ice that slides and collects large amounts of snow.

hard water: water containing lots of minerals.

herbs: plant used to flavor foods.

humidity: measurement of the weight of water in a specific volume of air.

humus: dark substance made up of decayed living things.

hydra: small freshwater tubular organism with a mouth surrounded by tentacles.

ice crystals: tiny forms made by freezing water vapor.

igneous: rock formed by great amounts of heat.

impressions: marks on a surface made by pressing into it.

infrared rays: waves of light that are just beyond red in the color spectrum but cannot be seen.

kernel: edible part of a nut.

lichen: small plant composed of a particular fungus that attaches itself to objects.

limestone: material consisting mainly of calcium carbonate from the remains of sea animals.

membrane: the layer around a cell or the round parts of a cell.

metamorphic: rocks that have undergone several changes in heat and pressure.

minerals: compounds that make up rocks.

molecule: smallest part of an element or compound capable of leading a separate existence.

mollusk: animal with a soft, segmented body.

nerve endings: ends of nerves that send messages to an animal's brain for interpretation.

nocturnal: active at night.

nut: hard fruit containing a seed.

opaque: material that does not let light pass or shine through.

orb web: garden spider web with spokelike formations.

orbit: path followed as objects circle around others.

organic matter: plant and animal decayed material.

oxidation: the union of one substance with air.

pheromones: chemicals given off outside the body by some animals.

photosynthesis: the process of making food from light.

pigment: coloring matter.

pistil: female part of a flower that has the stigma and produces seeds.

pollen: male spores of a plant.

pressure: the amount of force pressing on an area.

quad prints: prints made where animals leave four distinct prints as they bounce along.

recycle: reuse in a different form.

sap: juice that flows through a plant.

scales: thin, flat, hard plates that cover and protect some fish.

sedimentary: rocks formed by the matter left at the bottom of a liquid.

seed coat: coating or shell of a seed.

segment: section

sensory adaptation: senses in a living thing that try to figure out what to feel.

sepals: part of a flower outside the bud or underneath the open flower.

sheet web: spider web generally built indoors by house spiders and found in corners.

soil: top layer of earth in which plants grow.

stalactites: formations hanging down in caves made from the dripping of chemicals.

stalagmites: formations growing up in caves made from the dripping of chemicals.

stalk: the stem part of a plant.

stamen: the part of the flower where the pollen grows.

stratus clouds: low, foggy, spread-out clouds that may extend in flat layers and mean bad weather is ahead.

subsoil: dirt or soil just under the top layer of soil.

surface tension: force that keeps drops of liquid together.

swim bladder: organ in a fish that controls buoyancy by varying the amount and pressure of the air.

topsoil: top layer of soil rich in nutrients.

translucent: material that lets light pass through.

velocity: rate of speed or motion.

weathering: wearing away of the earth by wind and water.

Further Reading

Butterfield, Moira. *1000 Facts About the Earth* (New York: Kingfisher Books, 1992).

Cornell, Joseph. *Sharing the Joy of Nature* (Nevada City, CA: Dawn Publications, 1989).

Dekkers, Midas. *The Nature Book* (New York: Macmillan, 1988).

Elkington, John, Hailes, Julia, and Makover, Joel. *Going Green: A Kid's Handbook to Saving the Earth* (Kansas City, MO: Puffin Books, 1990).

Friend, Mari. *Discovering Nature's Secrets* (New York: Universe, 1992).

Grafton, Allison, and Levine, Shar. *Projects for a Healthy Planet: Simple Environmental Experiments for Kids* (New York: John Wiley & Sons, 1992).

Hann, Judith. *How Science Works* (New York: Reader's Digest Association, 1991).

Harlow, Rosie, and Morgan, Gareth. *175 Amazing Nature Experiments* (New York: Random House, 1991).

Headlam, Catherine. *Science Encyclopedia* (New York: Grisewood & Dempsey, 1993).

Herman, Marina Lachecki, and Passineau, Joseph F. *Teaching Kids to Love the Earth* (Duluth, MN: Pfeifer-Hamilton Publishers, 1991).

Hickman, Pamela M. *Bugwise* (Reading, MA: Addison Wesley, 1990).

Kohl, Maryann, and Potter, Jean. *ScienceArts* (Bellingham, WA: Bright Ring Publishing, 1993).

Mammana, Dennis. *The Night Sky* (Philadelphia, PA: Running Press, 1989).

McKeever, Susan. *Science Encyclopedia* (New York: Dorling Kindersley, 1993).

Mitchell, Andrew. *The Young Naturalist* (Tulsa, OK: EDC Publishing, 1982).

Pope, Joyce, and Whitfield, Dr. Philip. *Why Do Seasons Change?* (New York: Viking Kestrel 1987).

Roberts, Allen. *The Curiosity Club Kid's Nature Activity Book* (New York: John Wiley & Sons, 1992).

Robson, Pam, and Seller, Mick. *Science Workshop* (New York: Shooting Star Press, 1992).

Schwartz, Linda. *Earth Book for Kids* (Santa Barbara, CA: The Learning Works, 1990).

Seed, Deborah. *Water Science* (Reading, MA: Addison-Wesley, 1992).

Sheehan, Kathryn, and Waidner, Mary. *Earth Child* (Tulsa, OK: Council Oak Books, 1991).

Taylor, Barbara. *Green Thumbs Up!* (New York: Random House, 1992).

Tilgner, Linda. *Let's Grow: 72 Gardening Adventures with Children* (Pownal, VT: Sotrey Communications, 1988).

Walker, Lois. *Get Growing* (New York: John Wiley & Sons, 1993).

Webster, David. *Exploring Nature Around the Year: Spring* (Englewood Cliffs, NJ: Julian Messner, 1990).

Williams, John. *Projects with Air* (Milwaukee, WI: Gareth Stevens Children's Books, 1990).

Williams, John. *Projects with Color and Light* (Milwaukee, WI: Gareth Stevens Children's Books, 1990).

Williams, John. *Projects with Water* (Milwaukee, WI: Gareth Stevens Children's Books, 1990).

Wyatt, Valerie. *Weather Watch* (Reading, MA: Addison Wesley, 1990).

Activity Index